Famous Case His
Neurotrauma

Using a popular case history format, this book presents a scientific history of neurotrauma. It covers a range of well-known cases, including Roald Dahl, James Brady, and Walter Freeman to give insights into a variety of neurotrauma causes and effects, from aphasia and amnesia to lobotomy and mercury toxicity.

Cases are connected to clinical research methods, exploring how these methods have changed over time and illustrating how these cases are still relevant as we continue to learn about recovery from brain and spinal cord injuries. Focusing on individuals who survived their injuries beyond the acute phase, the book highlights the long-term behavioral effects of the injuries and provides estimates for prognoses and recovery pathways in acknowledgment of naturally occurring neuroregeneration. With helpful key term definitions, Matyas distinguishes fact from fiction to give an accurate account of a wide spectrum of cases and highlight what we can learn from them.

Famous Case Histories in Neurotrauma is valuable reading for students in behavioral neuroscience, clinical neuropsychology and related fields.

Jessica Matyas is the Chair of the Department of Psychology and Behavioral Sciences at Rochester University, located in Rochester, Michigan, with research and teaching experience. She has previously published in the area of spinal cord injury and is an authority in this aspect of CNS trauma.

Famous Case Histories in Neurotrauma

What Neuroscience Continues to Learn from Survivors

Jessica Matyas

Routledge
Taylor & Francis Group

NEW YORK AND LONDON

First published 2021
by Routledge
52 Vanderbilt Avenue, New York, NY 10017

and by Routledge
2 Park Square, Milton Park, Abingdon, Oxon, OX14 4RN

Routledge is an imprint of the Taylor & Francis Group, an informa business

Library of Congress Cataloging-in-Publication Data
Names: Matyas, Jessica, author.
Title: Famous case histories in neurotrauma / Jessica Matyas.
Description: New York, NY : Routledge, 2021. | Includes
bibliographical references and index.
Identifiers: LCCN 2020014274 (print) | LCCN 2020014275
(ebook) | ISBN 9780367442859 (hardback) | ISBN
9780367442835 (paperback) | ISBN 9781003008798 (ebook)
Subjects: LCSH: Nervous system–Wounds and injuries–Case
studies. | Nervous system–Wounds and injuries–Patients–
Rehabilitation–Case studies.
Classification: LCC RD593 .M386 2021 (print) | LCC RD593
(ebook) | DDC 617.4/8044–dc23
LC record available at https://lccn.loc.gov/2020014274
LC ebook record available at https://lccn.loc.gov/2020014275

ISBN: 978-0-367-44285-9 (hbk)
ISBN: 978-0-367-44283-5 (pbk)
ISBN: 978-1-003-00879-8 (ebk)

Typeset in Sabon
by Swales & Willis, Exeter, Devon, UK

Printed in the United Kingdom
by Henry Ling Limited

For all those currently living with the after-effects of brain and spinal cord injuries, whose prognoses were so grim it took away their hope: There is *always* hope. Keep moving forward!

Contents

Acknowledgments

In addition to the individuals and families of those who allowed me to use their remarkable stories in this collection of case histories, I'd like to especially thank my loved ones for supporting me throughout the production of this book. A special thank you to my dad for reminding me that I should keep doing what makes me happy, to my mother for inspiring me to study neurotrauma in the first place, my sister for always being excited to hear a weird or gross new story, and my friends for putting up with my constant 'does this sound okay' proofreads. You guys are the best!

Chapter 1

'What Could Possibly Go Wrong?'

An Introduction to Neurotrauma

Introduction

The field of neuroscience is among the youngest of sciences, and arguably one of the most heavily interdisciplinary sciences, integrating biology, chemistry, medicine, and psychology together into a single broad field. While its origins and official start as a unique field is debated, we can reach a consensus on the fact that many of the early findings in neuroscience arose as a result of unique and, at times, confusing individual cases of injury and illness. In particular, traumatic injuries that would traditionally have been fatal now are addressed by rapidly improving technology and medicine, allowing individuals to not only survive, but recover from damage to the brain and spinal cord, an area now known as neurotrauma. By acknowledging these ever-changing aspects of the field, we are able to revisit historical cases with new information and new ways of thinking, shedding light on mysteries that at the time were unexplainable. From anthropological records of trephination, or the boring of holes in the living skull, to the world's most famous head injury, Phineas Gage, and modern findings such as those of James Brady's gunshot wound and Christopher Reeve's equestrian accident, we will explore the history of neurotrauma as a subset of neuroscience, and how these remarkable case studies helped to shape the field as we know it, further connecting these to both traditional and currently used research methods.

Disclaimers/Words of Warning

If you are at all familiar with cinematic representations of mental hospitals, you likely hold an opinion that traditional treatment methods were somewhat barbaric. However, it is important to note that the major goal of any respectable science is to help others. The treatments that may seem awful or inhumane to us now were, at the time, the best options available to medicine and psychology. If you are in a field of science yourself, then you are all too familiar with the idea that we must do the best we can with what we are given. This is precisely what the professionals in these case histories did: The best with what they had at the time. It is all but guaranteed that in the next century, our successors will look back at our current methods in horror, calling us as barbaric as we now call the early twentieth-century physicians. Therefore, please keep in mind throughout the following text that true malice and intent to harm was extremely rare in this field, and that everything was done with the hopes that it would be helpful to others. We just have a long track record of getting things wrong. Such is the nature of learning.

Case studies in trauma are innumerable, as humans as a whole continue to find new and unusual ways to hurt ourselves. As such, only a small collection could be discussed in this volume. Those included here fit into a set of criteria, including first and foremost that the individuals or groups being discussed had to have survived their initial injuries or insults and lived for a significant amount of time afterwards. While comparisons will be made to certain disease states, the present cases also are exclusive to sudden trauma, whether brought on by direct impact or chemical/biological means. Therefore, an ischemic stroke fits the criteria for a case of neurotrauma; however, a degenerative disease like Alzheimer's disease is too far-reaching and slow-moving, despite being equally as important to study.

There will certainly be aspects of each case that get missed or omitted, and for that I request forgiveness. Each of the cases discussed within this text are deserving of entire volumes on their own (and some do indeed already have books published about their cases). The summary versions here therefore have a different goal than typical case history texts. We will explore the cases themselves, the primary effects of each injury, and some of the more unexpected effects that may go overlooked at first glance.

Basics of Neuroanatomy

Before diving into the first major case history, it may be helpful to go over key concepts and terminology that will be discussed later on. For those who are new to neurotrauma, this will hopefully be helpful for a head start on the materials. If you are experienced in the field, on the other hand, forgive the brevity of this section and enjoy the hidden jokes that may be peppered throughout. But for all intents and purposes, consider this section to be the extreme nut-shell version of an introduction to neuroscience. Sources for the following material were collected from various textbooks that are commonly used in biopsychology and behavioral neuroscience courses (Kolb & Wishaw, 2009; Kalat, 2013, 2019; Pinel & Barnes, 2018).

The Four (or Five) Cortical Lobes. As a whole, the large, dense neocortex is what makes humans what we are, with more convolutions (wrinkles) and connections than comparable species. Based on general function, the cortex can be broken down into four 'lobes', though a fifth can be argued depending on how deep into the brain you would like to explore (see Figure 1.1).

At the very back of the brain is the occipital lobe, whose role is for processing vision. Information passes from the eyes through the optic nerves, is processed in the occipital lobe, and then sent onward through the ventral and dorsal streams to other brain areas, which determine 'what' and 'where' something is, respectively. The ventral stream travels through the temporal lobe, located on either side of the brain behind the temporal bone (where the temples are on your head). This lobe primarily handles hearing, but also plays major roles in memory. The dorsal stream travels upwards to the parietal lobe at the top rear of the brain, which serves as the perception center. This region interprets information from the entire body and works with the frontal lobe to control the motor cortex. The frontal lobe itself, taking up the largest space in the front half of the brain, is the last to receive most information, and also the last brain area to mature, typically not completing its development until the early 20s, if at all. As such, this area is quite fragile, especially affected by drugs like alcohol, and controls functions like the regulation of behaviors and interpretation of abstract concepts. Arguably, the frontal lobe is the brain area that makes us who we are as individuals, as we will see in Chapter 3.

The debatable 'fifth lobe', often declared as more of a midbrain region because of its positioning between the cortex and 'lower' brain areas, is the limbic system, the emotional control center (see Figure 1.2).

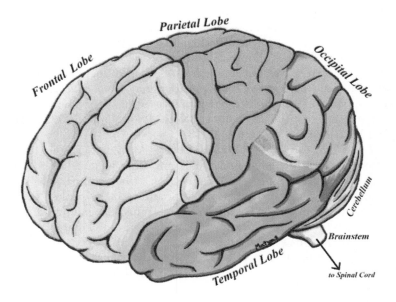

Figure 1.1 The four main lobes of the human neocortex: The occipital lobe, home of visual processing; the temporal lobe, home of auditory and memory processing; the parietal lobe, seat of sensation and perception; and the frontal lobe, involved in cognition, personality, and the regulation of behaviors.

It includes the sub-structures of the hippocampus, the memory-critical area, the amygdala, the fear and anger area, the septum, a calming area that only coincidentally shares a name with nasal cartilage, and the cingulate gyrus, a deep cortical ridge implicated in pervasive emotional disorders. Other important cortical regions include the sensorimotor cortex, whose sensory ridge lies at the edge of the parietal lobe and its motor ridge at the back of the frontal lobe. The cerebellum at the base of the skull below the occipital lobe assists with balance and coordination, as well as habit-learning, and contains more cells than the rest of the brain combined. The basal ganglia deep within the center of the brain also controls motor function, but in a different manner than other regions, such as with voluntary

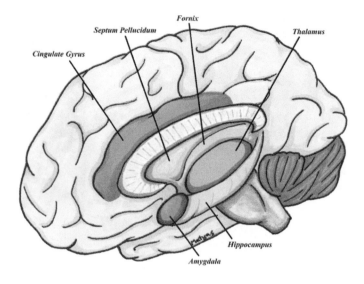

Figure 1.2 The limbic system and medial cortex, with emphasis on the hippocampus, amygdala, and cingulate gyrus. While known as the system that regulates emotions, both in identifying and expressing emotions, this area is also deeply involved in memory processing, particularly for the formation of new, conscious memories.

stepping and maintaining posture.[1] The thalamus at the very central core of the brain is what I personally like to call the 'bureaucrat of the brain', as it collects, organizes, and sends out all information coming into and going out of the brain. Finally, the brainstem and spinal cord consist of massive bundles of white matter, acting as electrical highways to send information rapidly, including vital organ function, autonomic regulation, and all other bodily senses. Trauma to the spinal cord, which we will discuss in a later chapter, is quite survivable, however, trauma to the brainstem is very often fatal.[2]

Lateralization and Directionality. In order to navigate where in the brain we are, neurologists use anatomic directions based around key areas (see Figure 1.3).

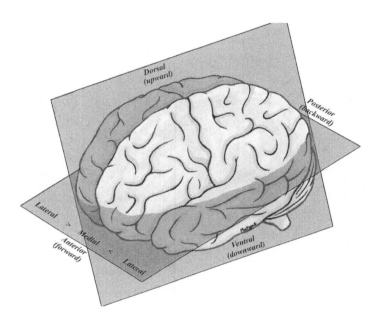

Figure 1.3 Anatomical directions in the human brain, showing the anterior/posterior axis, which runs from the front to the back of the brain, the medial/lateral axis, which runs from the center to the outer sides of the brain, and the dorsal/ventral axis, which runs to the top and bottom of the brain. Continuation of anatomical directions to the spinal cord adapt to include rostral/caudal directions running toward the brain (also called proximal) or toward the tailbone, the dorsal/ventral axis shifting to refer to the back or front of the body, and the medial/lateral axis remaining the same.

When doing stereotactic surgery, which utilizes precise equipment measuring three directions on a micrometer scale, fusion lines on the skull such as bregma and lambda are used as standard locations, which remain relatively stable from person to person. From these points, we can go laterally, or to the side, medially toward the center, anterior toward the front, or posterior toward the back. In the vertical direction, the top of the head and down along the spine is dorsal (imagine if humans were to have a dorsal fin), while ventral is the bottom of the brain or the front of the spinal column, in the direction of the lungs and airways (as if 'venting' air). Cross-sections such as those used for histology or demonstration can be done coronally, or across the crown of the head (as if you were looking through the face and into the brain), sagittal, which is lengthwise from front to back, or horizontal, which is more top-down or bottom-up view. Finally, when looking at the spinal column or animal models, whose postures are far different from humans, rostral refers to toward the head and caudal refers to toward the tail.

Maintaining Health. In the absence of major illnesses or traumatic damage, the brain does a rather good job of taking care of itself. Proper nutrition and health, including high antioxidant foods like dark colored fruits and vegetables, can further support brain health. Among the many ways the brain maintains its own health are the meninges and the blood brain barrier (BBB). The meninges are three layered membranes that cover the entire brain like its own personal shrink wrap. The outermost layer is the dura mater, meaning 'tough mother', named for its strength and resistance. The innermost is the pia mater, meaning 'gentle mother', which is extremely fragile compared to the dura, and adheres directly to the brain's surface. In between the two is the subarachnoid space. Named for its resemblance to spider webs, fibers weave across the gap between the dura and pia maters, embedded with blood vessels and circulating cerebrospinal fluid (CSF). This directly connects to the other major brain-health system, the BBB.

When producing and taking drugs or medicines, the route of administration is a key factor for determining how effective or dangerous a drug can be. It also is necessary for determining whether or not the drug can have an effect in the brain. This is because the BBB selectively filters out many compounds, preventing them from entering the brain in the first place. Typically, lipid soluble compounds and small molecules are able to pass through the barrier, while larger molecules cannot, but may enter if they are actively transported through by specialized protein pumps. Pharmaceutical developers can use this to their advantage by generating formulas that specifically do or do not pass the BBB, such as loperamide, commonly used as an anti-diarrhea drug, which is technically an opiate, but is unable to pass into the brain. The system can, of course, be compromised and has some natural weak points. The cribiform plate, a structure between the nasal sinuses and forebrain, is the weakest point of the BBB, and a potential focus of future research on toxic damage due to recreational drug use or infectious disease.

Cells of the CNS. Most non-scientists are already aware that nerves within the brain and spinal cord are responsible for the communication and signaling therein. Of course, the details of CNS function are far more complex, but to begin we must start with the cells themselves. When contained within the skull or spinal column, nerves are called neurons, and are supported by another class of cells called glia, from the Latin word for 'glue'. Originally thought to simply hold together the neural network, glia are now regarded as just as important, or at times *more* important, than neurons. This class can be broken down into more detailed cell types including astrocytes, microglia, oligo-dendrocytes, and more. While each cell type has its major responsibilities, they overlap significantly and may differ in function depending on where they are found and in what shape they are in at the time (particularly with microglia).

Beginning with neurons, the gold standard model of a neuron is based on the Hodgkin-Huxley model from the Giant Squid Axon. Not all neurons operate this exact way, but the model serves as a good representative for general neuronal function. Signaling travels in one direction only, from the dendrites, or branches,[3] above the cell's body through a single axon and out the terminal buttons on the far end (Figure 1.4).

The dendrites receive stimulation from other cells, and communicate that to the cell body, or soma, the command center for that particular cell. Here, the neurotransmitters are packaged into vesicles, water balloon-like spheres made of the same phospholipid bilayer that the rest of the cell membrane is. Vesicles travel along microtubules in the axon to the terminal buttons, and when the signal is given to send an outgoing transmission, they fuse with the cell membrane and release their contents into the synaptic cleft, a gap between one cell's terminals and the next one's dendrites. From there, the process can begin all over again. This is of course an oversimplified version of the chemical aspect of neuronal communication, while the electrical aspect is more focused on the membrane.

At the neck of the neuron's axon, or Axon Hillock, an electrical signal begins and passes along the exposed membranes until it reaches the terminals. Myelin, a fatty compound produced by specialized glial cells, wraps around the axon to provide insulation, protect it from damage, and speed up the electrical signal (see subset of Figure 1.4). Packets of glia are interrupted by nodes of

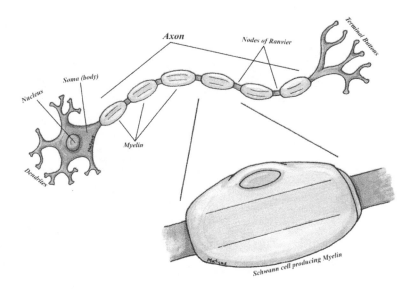

Figure 1.4 Illustration of a typical neuron and its major structures, including the dendrites, cell body, axon, myelin, and terminals. Enlarged inset shows a myelinating Schwann cell, which are found primarily in the peripheral nervous system.

Ranvier, small exposed surfaces of the neuron's cell membrane. The nodes allow saltatory Conduction, a sort of 'jumping' of the action potential from one gap to the next, which multiplies the speed of transmission. Loss of myelin, as seen in many diseases as well as after traumatic injury, slows things down and can produce a number of unpleasant symptoms such as loss of motor control, mental scanning, and others. If too much of the cell membrane is exposed after myelin loss, this can also lead to aberrant, or incorrect, signaling, leading to pain and spasticity.

The first of many glial cells are those which produce myelin: Oligodendrocytes in the CNS and Schwann cells in the peripheral nervous system (PNS) (Figure 1.5).

Schwann cells produce a growth-promoting form of myelin, but can only act on a single cell at a time. Oligodendrocytes, on the other hand, can myelinate several cells at once, as well as help

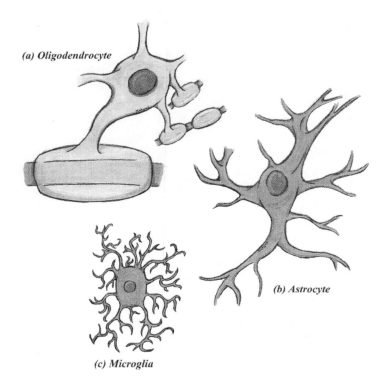

Figure 1.5 Stylized illustrations of three types of glial cells: (a) Oligodendrocyte, a myelin producing cell in the central nervous system; (b) Astrocyte, a multifunctional cell involved in everything from the introduction of nutrients to the disposal of waste products and regulation of the blood brain barrier; and (c) Microglia, a major cell of the immune system within the CNS, involved in both inflammatory and anti-inflammatory processes.

synchronize their activity, but this type of myelin is growth-inhibiting in order to prevent incorrect connections in the event of damage to an axon. Current studies geared toward improving myelin function, such as for spinal cord injuries or multiple sclerosis, are exploring whether Schwann cells can be transplanted to the CNS or if oligodendrocytes can be encouraged to restore and reorganize the myelin of surviving CNS neurons; cell transplantation is also being tested to see if the replacement of lost and dying cells can restore myelin.

The next type of glial cell to discuss is quite literally the 'star of the show', as its name directly translates to 'star cell', the astrocyte (Figure 1.5b). Named for its starburst-like shape, these cells are often larger than standard neurons, and have a wide range of functions. Astrocytes operate within the blood-brain barrier, bringing nutrients into the brain, attacking invaders like pathogens, moderating the immune system, and even forming scar tissue to prevent damage from spreading. This last function, however, may occasionally act against our best interests, as the glial scar formed after traumatic injuries also prevents neurons from growing through the barrier and reconnecting. Research in this area is exploring how the scar can be removed or dissolved after formation[4] to promote endogenous recovery, or that which takes place naturally within the body.

Working in tandem with the astrocytes are microglia, named such for their diminutive size. Often much smaller than even the cell body of a neuron, microglia are essentially immune-system cells (Figure 1.5c). They change their body shapes depending on what function they are fulfilling at the time. If inactive, microglia are at their simplest and most unremarkable, known as quiescent or ramified. If activated or bushy, they are basically on the clock and working. Their major responsibilities include removing debris and managing inflammation with both pro- and anti-inflammatory morphologies. The pro-inflammatory shape, called M1, boosts the body's ability to fight off pathogens. However, as in the rest of the body, too much inflammation can be a dangerous thing, particularly when the confines of the skull give a limited space for expansion. So, there is a large body of research now geared toward shifting microglia to their M2 anti-inflammatory phenotypes, which may have a dramatic effect on recovery from trauma.

Other types of glial cells, like radial glia, assist with migration of cells during the development of the brain, and while they do not get as much publicity and attention as other glia, they are no less important. As with the balance of neurotransmitters, the balance between neurons and glia are critical to healthy functions within the brain and spinal cord. Some areas possess far more glia than neurons, while others are more neuron-dense, as in the cerebellum.

Basics of Neural Signaling

Neural signaling is a term that applies to how cells of the central nervous system (CNS) communicate with one another, including both electrical and chemical systems. Its study has been of interest since the early days of neuroscience when Golgi and Cajal separately identified ways to examine cellular structures and confirmed that neurons are not in direct contact with one another, but must use other ways of transmitting information.[5] Eventually, research from such pioneers as Galvani and Sperry would confirm both the electrical and chemical influences, respectively, while the famed Hodgkin and Huxley experiments with giant squid axons identified the major functions of the neuron's main highway, the axon. While we have a great overall picture now of the basic way that the CNS communicates with itself, we are still discovering many of the finer details. The following section is only the basic nuts and bolts of what is needed to explore the cases to follow.

Hebb's Law and Neural Pruning. All students of neuroscience are expected to remember rule one about neural signaling. Hebb's law, named for its postulator, states that cells that fire together wire together. This means that the more frequently that two cells communicate with one another, the stronger their connection, and the more resistant that connection is against damage. The principle can be further paired with the 'use it or lose it' motto of many physical therapists,[6] as those connections that are not used tend to remain weak at best and may be susceptible to neural pruning. During the typical course of development, the young brain produces many cells and many connections, but not all of these will be helpful. Therefore, neural pruning, like the pruning of tree branches that are not useful to the health of the plant, strengthens the remaining branches. Such trimming is seen as its own form of growth, as the age at which pruning is at its peak is also the age at which learning may be considered to be at its peak, throughout grade school ages. Paired together, while unused connections are being pruned, those being used are being strengthened, and the inhibition of either of these systems is detrimental to healthy brain development.

Electrical 'Firing'. When discussing neural signaling, we say 'firing' in the same sense as one fires a gun: Launching a missile forward, but in this case the missile is an electrochemical signal. At rest, the cell maintains an internal charge of about -70 mV.

When stimulated past a minimum threshold (the absolute threshold), channels open to allow positive ions to rush into the cell, and the resulting surge of activity, called an action potential, continues along the length of the cell membrane. Due to the nature of the reaction, the action potential happens at full strength or not at all, known as the All or None Principle. Further, instead of a single surge traveling the length of the axon, the reaction is repeated at every exposed point along the cell membrane, ensuring that it will remain at full strength regardless of how long the axon is. The presence of myelin speeds the process up even more by ensheathing the axon and leaving only Nodes of Ranvier exposed, as discussed above. Quickly, the signal reaches the terminals at the end of the line, and trigger the release of the chemical communicators, Neurotransmitters.

Neurotransmitters. The specialized chemicals known as neurotransmitters do everything from increase and decrease brain activity to regulate one another and control the entire body. They are found not only in the brain and spinal cord, but also in the organs, muscles, and gut.[7] Dozens have been identified, but only a handful do the majority of the work. Among those that get the most attention, dopamine is popularly known as 'the only thing you really love', which stimulates feelings of pleasure as well as aiding in voluntary motor control, but in excess can contribute to psychosis. Gamma-aminobutyric acid (GABA) is inhibitory, decreasing overall activity and producing a calming feeling, and can be boosted by drugs like alcohol and benzodiazepines (e.g., Xanax), and to a lesser degree, chamomile. Glutamate is the most common excitatory neurotransmitter, which increases overall activity, and has implications in a wide array of symptoms such as cognitive function, chronic stress, and psychosis. Acetylcholine is the most common whole-body neurotransmitter, even present in the muscles, which can be both inhibitory and excitatory, and may have an active role in symptoms of Alzheimer's disease. Finally, what I personally like to call the 'problem child' of the neurotransmitters, serotonin. Often targeted by antidepressants, serotonin does have an active role in emotional regulation, though it has further actions with memory as well as digestion, being the primary neurotransmitter of the enteric nervous system in the intestines. An imbalance in any single type of neurotransmitter can, and often does, wreak havoc on the brain's overall function, and we are only beginning to understand the details of how they work.

The Synapse. Communication between two neurons does not occur through direct contact. Instead, information passes through a space between two points, like words passing between people while talking to one another. The gap between a sending neuron's terminal buttons and the receiving neuron's dendrites is called the synaptic cleft or synaptic gap, while the entire system itself comprises the synapse (Figure 1.6).

Calcium enters the terminal button, or pre-synaptic membrane, leading the cell to release its neurotransmitters into the cleft. If the neurotransmitters pass across the gap to the post-synaptic membrane, they may then bind to receptor ligands, which specifically bind to particular neurotransmitters,[8] and the signal can continue onward through the next cell. However, if the neurotransmitters do not bind to the post-synaptic receptors, then they may either be broken down by enzymes within the cleft or taken back up into the presynaptic cell by reuptake channels. Excess

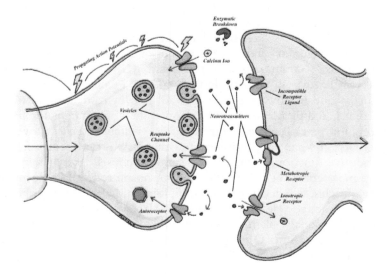

Figure 1.6 Stylized illustration of a synapse, featuring representations of vesicles, post-synaptic receptors (ionotropic and metabotropic), autoreceptors, reuptake channels, and enzymatic breakdown of neurotransmitters.

neurotransmitters may also bind to autoreceptors on the presynaptic membrane and serve as a feedback signal to stop releasing the compound. If at any point these processes get thrown off-balance, then there may be significant mental and emotional effects as a result. For instance, high levels of activity of the enzyme acetylcholinesterase are related to reduced activity in the basal forebrain in those with Alzheimer's disease, overly high levels of dopamine in the frontal lobe are related to psychosis, and excessive reuptake activity in serotonin and norepinephrine neurons are related to emotional disorders like depression.

Post-Traumatic Terminology

The following sections are intended as short-hand references for those who either have not been introduced to the basics of neurotrauma or who, like myself, tend to work in such a way that you find yourself at a loss for the meaning of a word you already know but cannot think of, requiring you to look it up. These are by no means the full definitions of any of the terms, but can act as quick reminders of the key points as they relate to the stories ahead.

Acute vs Chronic   Ranges of time post-trauma. Acute is commonly accepted as the time immediately after an insult until the initial shock has faded, which then transitions into sub-acute. Chronic refers to the slowing down of recovery processes and continues throughout the lifespan.

Encephalitis   Translating to within the skull swelling; inflammation within the central nervous system as a result of infection.

Epicenter   The exact site of a lesion or insult; often where the damage originated.

Glial Scar   A physical barrier that forms at the site of insult from glial cells as an attempt to prevent the secondary cascade from spreading; initially protective, but inhibits new growth and recovery.

Insult   General term for any damage done to the body, particularly the CNS; may include a stroke, tumor, seizure, chemical damage, or direct trauma.

Lesion   Missing or damaged tissue at the center of an injury or insult.

Penumbra   The damaged tissue at the borders of a lesion's epicenter; often contains still living cells and tissues, and can be used as a potential therapeutic target.

Secondary Cascade   Continual damage that occurs after the initial insult has taken place; can include scarring, continued cell death, metabolic changes, and other undesired effects.

Additional Terms and Definitions

Anterior   Toward the front of the brain.

Atrophy   Shrinkage or die-back of cells and tissue over time; may be due to damage, illness, or lack of use and input.

Caudal   Meaning 'to the tail', in the direction of the feet when discussing the spinal cord or animal models.

Cephalic   A suffix referring to the head and its contents.

Cognitive/Cognition   Thought processes and mental activities.

Contralaterality   The tendency for one side of the brain to control the opposite side of the body.

Convolutions   The 'wrinkles' in the cortex that correlate to cognitive abilities.

Corpus Callosum   Meaning 'massive body', the white matter tracts connecting the left and right hemispheres of the brain.

Cranium   The skull.

Distal   Far away from, as in distal limbs like the hands and feet.

Dorsal   Toward the top of the brain or back of the spinal cord.

-Ectomy   A suffix referring to the removal of tissue, as opposed to -otomy being a cut without removal.

Fasciculus   A bundle of white matter fibers connecting two or more brain areas.

Fissure   A large sulcus or chasm in the brain's wrinkles.

Ganglion/Ganglia   A dense group of peripheral nerves or a group of CNS nuclei connected with the cortex, thalamus, and brainstem, such as the basal ganglia; also, a bundle of nerves bridging the CNS to the PNS, as in the ventral and dorsal root ganglia.

Gyrus/Gyri   Hills or raised portions of the cortex.

Hemisphere   One of the large halves of the brain; the left hemisphere typically controls logic and speech while the right controls emotion and perception. Added note: A person cannot be 'right-brained' or 'left-brained'. Dominance between hemispheres refers to which half is in control of speech and conscious function.

Lateral   To the side of; more lateral areas are farther from the center of the body/brain.

Medial   To the middle of; more medial areas are closer to the center of the body/brain.

Nucleus/Nuclei   A dense group of neurons or a central region of interest, such as the arcuate nucleus of the hypothalamus.

-Otomy   A suffix referring to the cutting of tissue, but not removal, as opposed to -ectomy.

Posterior   Behind or toward the back of the brain.

Proximal   Closer to; for example, proximal to a lesion is closer to its location.

Resection   The act of cutting out a portion of tissue, such as a tumor.

Rostral   Toward the head when discussing the spinal cord or animal models.

Sulcus/Sulci   Depressions or chasms in the cortex.

Ventral   Toward the front of the body or bottom of the brain.

Notes

1 Though not shown in the figure, this structure is located mid-brain, generally adjacent to the hippocampus and located lateral to, or to the sides of, the thalamus.

2 In general, the closer a spinal injury is to the brain, the more severe and life-threatening the situation is.

3 You may notice a trend for there to be tree references and terminology in common with arborists. This is not a coincidence. Many terms are named such because of direct parallels they share with the structures of plants and trees. For example, the way that existing branches of both neurons and trees thicken and thrive when weaker ones are cut back. Life is beautiful that way.

4 An important note here is that glial scar removal is best done *after* scar formation; the formation of the scar should not be prevented. Prevention of the scar has been found to aggravate traumatic damage and worsen functional outcomes.

5 Golgi and Cajal would share a Nobel Prize for their discoveries, but, ironically, hated one another and spent their acceptance speeches criticizing the other's works.

6 The muscle systems are not so disconnected from the nervous system as one might think. Aside from motor neuron diseases like Amyotrophic Lateral Sclerosis (ALS), muscle wasting is a side effect of

many neurological conditions, and the growth and atrophy of muscles parallel that of neural connections.

7   The gut has such a highly detailed nervous system of its own that it has been called the third bodily nervous system; the brain and spine being central, the body and organs peripheral, and the gut the enteric. The relationship between the gut and brain is now a hot button topic gaining traction in research, and may well find its way into a future edition of this book.

8   There are exceptions to this rule, as some receptor ligands are unable to tell the difference between two similarly shaped compounds. Pharmaceutical sciences have taken advantage of this by generating artificial compounds that mimic natural neurotransmitters, such as morphine and other opiates. It is essentially the neurological version of 'if you can't make your own, store bought is fine'.

Chapter 2

'Bone Windows'
Trephination and the Modern Craniotomy

Anthropological Records

Word of mouth travels fast in general, but faster still when the story being told has an air of magic and mystery to it. So, when human skulls were unearthed bearing large, hand-carved holes in them and signs of healing around the edges of the damaged bone, theories occasionally turned to mystical explanations. Perhaps the unlucky souls were victims of a shamanic practices or an intense form of exorcism? If a demon were trapped within someone's brain making them sick, then the best course would obviously have been to release them through the skull. Or, maybe the practice was related to the archaic concept of bloodletting, by evacuating bad fluids from within the body. But then again, sometimes the truth is stranger than fiction, and just maybe, thousands of years ago humans had discovered a way to relieve certain neurological conditions with the use of a sharpened stone or a hand-powered drill.

In the mid-nineteenth century, the explorer Ephraim George Squier received a Peruvian skull as a gift, which featured a small square hole cut into it, likely the result of a procedure known as 'trephination' or 'trepanation'.[1] Damage to an anthropological or archaeology specimen was not unexpected, yet this one looked different. The hole had been cut very precisely, and there were signs of healing around the edges of the bone, indicating that the skull's former owner had survived for some length of time, at least a couple of weeks, after the hole had been cut (Gross, 2009) (Figure 2.1).

At the time, a comparable procedure done in hospitals by trained professionals would result in death nine times out of ten, so it was that much more surprising not only that this person had survived an ancient version of it, but also that they were far

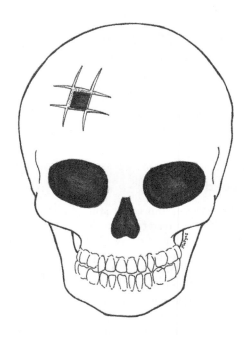

Figure 2.1 Approximate location and size of the trephined hole in Squier's Peruvian skull. Lines adjacent to the opening indicate where a sharp object likely cut into, but not through, the bone.

from the only person to have survived such an operation. Squier began communicating with colleagues on the matter, and estimated that as many as 70–90 percent of people may have survived ancient trephination procedures, a far cry from the then-modern 10–30 percent survival rate. Skulls showing signs of successful trephination were found not only in South America, but also in France, Africa, China, Rome, Iran, and the Bismarck Archipelago (Mallin & Rathbun, 1976; Clower & Finger, 2001; Watters, 2007; Gross, 2009; Faria, 2013). Through records traced back through the Neolithic period, and based on the total number of skulls found in some areas, it was estimated that 5 percent of the whole population had received trephinations (Bandelier, 1904; Faria, 2015).

In communication with Squier, localization expert Pierre Paul Broca, who would later become famous for the discovery of a language-center in the left hemisphere of the brain, examined the Incan skull as well as others, determining the level of bone healing as well as signs of inflammation. Broca concluded not only that the holes had been intended as a form of surgical intervention, but that they may have had legitimate medical validation behind them (Clower & Finger, 2001). There were no apparent differences between laterality among the brains, meaning that the holes were just as common on the left side as the right. Had the holes been made through violence or as battle wounds, significantly more would have been found on the left sides of men's skulls as a result of right-handed attackers. While many trephined skulls did show signs of fracture, indicating the removal of bone as an emergency treatment for head trauma, the original Peruvian skull did not, suggesting that there were other signs and symptoms that these cultures would use to indicate that trephination was required.

The question of just why trephinations were the selected option has been attributed to spiritual or sensational reasons, such as excising demons (suspected to cause epilepsy) and 'resurrecting' the dead by restoring consciousness to head-injured people (Clower & Finger, 2001; Faria, 2015). Yet within the sensational reason lies a thread of logic, and a scientifically sound concept. Hippocrates, known as the father of modern medicine, described methods for trephination, even advising against doing the procedure near a suture, or fusion point in the bones of the skull, as this would be disastrous for the patient (Gross, 2009). Though the idea of releasing 'bad blood' remained, the primary goal of trephining was to relieve symptoms in those who had sustained a trauma to the head, which often results in seizures, as well as swelling and inflammation. Unlike the rest of the body, when there is swelling within the brain and spinal cord, the structures of the skeleton do not expand to accommodate the increased volume, and pressure begins to build up. This pressure can then increase the amount of damage already done, so relieving the pressure as soon as possible is critical to recovery. Without access to modern medicines like steroids and anti-inflammatories, the next best thing was to simply create an opening for the pressure to be released from. This opening could be created by scraping with a stone or flint, carving a groove, boring with a saw-like tool, or cutting the edges of the hole with straight lines as seen on Squier's Peruvian skull. In all cases, great care would be taken to avoid cutting into the brain itself. Only the skull was targeted for successful trephination.

As researchers continued to search for explanations for the trephined skulls, they noted that the location of many trephined holes were found over brain areas contributing to movement, which are associated with Jacksonian epilepsy, lending credence to therapeutic theories on trephination (Horsley, 1888). Broca also noted that many of these procedures seemed to be done on infants, who show increased incident rates of spontaneous seizure activity that tends to resolve over time, as opposed to true epilepsy (Clower & Finger, 2001). Boring the hole in a young person's skull was assuredly easier than doing so on adult skulls, and there would have been smoother recovery due to the patients' young ages. More adult cases found in other regions showed evidence of trephination to treat depressed fractures, in which shards of bone or pooling of blood could cause further damage to the brain (Bandelier, 1904; Mallin & Rathbun, 1976; Watters, 2007). Different cultures had various methods for trephination, such as rinsing wounds in coconut water or administering coca, the plant from which cocaine is derived, prior to the procedure to reduce pain.[2] Many had specialized tools to be used, including the exclusive use of obsidian glass or the development of specialized drills and saws.

Some level of spirituality was retained despite the apparent logic of the procedure, as rituals often accompanied trephination and portions of resected skull were often saved and worn as talismans, supposedly to ward off the demons that caused the seizures in the first place (Bandelier, 1904; Clower & Finger, 2001). Nonetheless, great care was taken throughout and even after creating the bone window. If the window was small enough, there was no major need to replace it, though larger trephinations may have necessitated the application of a fragment of gourd or metal plates to protect the brain in absence of its normal bone (Bandelier, 1904; Collado-Vázquez & Carrillo, 2014). Post-procedure, the wounds were kept clean, and full recovery could be expected within a number of weeks.

To some level, it seems surprising that researchers would be surprised by the discovery of trephination, given that so many cultures actively practiced it at the times of Squier's receipt of the

Peruvian skull. However, in the developed world of western Europe, a long history of documenting the negative side effects and ridiculing spiritualistic explanations led to resistance to the idea of boring holes in one's skull voluntarily. Renaissance artist Hieronymus Bosch, known for his depictions of hellscapes and torture, famously painted a piece entitled 'Extraction of the Stone of Madness', which depicted a then-modern trephination performed by a man with a funnel on his head while a priest and a woman with a book on her head stand nearby. Coupled with an increased rate of infection due to lax sanitary practices, trephination became an abhorred idea associated with barbaric torture. The procedure eventually faded in popularity, though never truly vanished, remaining in cultures with limited access to newly developed treatments, and later resurged when we discovered the benefits of decompression through medical and surgical interventions.

Craniotomies

After the initial horror of realizing that we as humans used to carve into a person's skull while they were still alive and sometimes even still awake, it's only slightly less disturbing to learn that we still do so. Methods have been significantly more refined of course, and the procedure is only performed by trained medical professionals. Renamed craniotomy, as it removes a portion of the cranium, it is considered to be a last resort intervention for swelling that does not respond to anti-inflammatories, massive bleeding, and removal of tumors (Kjellberg & Prieto, 1971; Zabramski et al., 1998; Gnanalingham et al., 2002). The expansion of decompressive craniotomy resurged in the 1970s as an emergency treatment for people with head trauma, including military personnel (soldiers and veterans) and other victims of traumatic brain injury. While mortality levels for emergency decompressive craniotomy remain high, this is likely due to its use in high-risk patients already considered to be moribund, or near-death. For soldiers in the field of battle, much like in centuries-old cases of trephination, cranial burr holes may be used to expose and remove life-threatening hemorrhage, carefully localized and executed based on such signs as an uneven pupillary reflex or enlarged pupil (Donovan et al., 2006). In cases of severe edema (swelling), bore holes could be made around the perimeter of the area to be removed, and specialized saws cut between the holes without damaging the underlying dura mater. The bone flap that was removed could then be stored in a bone bank or sterilized and kept for later replacement up to three months after the initial craniotomy to be replaced after the swelling had gone down (Kjellberg & Prieto, 1971). For those who survived the initial danger of their injuries, the replacement of the bone flap provided positive outcomes as well as a good aesthetic appearance with minimal distortion of the head's natural shape. Later adaptations to the procedure included storing the bone flap within the patient's own body to maintain the health of the bone, or using artificial means of cranioplasty, such as restoring the structure of the skull with titanium plates or methyl-methacrylate, a bone cement used in orthopedics (Faleiro et al., 2008).

Aside from acute trauma, there are other instances where craniotomy can be considered, such as the presence of a tumor or vascular lesion that must be removed. Depending on the location of such an insult, craniotomy can be performed in various regions of the skull. In an orbitozygomatic craniotomy, called such because of its location above the orbit (eye) and along the zygomatic arch (Figure 2.2), the person lays with their head back, the bone window is carefully made, and the brain can then be gently manipulated[3] (Zabramski et al., 1998). This approach allows access to such regions as the parasellar region where the pituitary gland is located, the cavernous sinus and its associated cranial nerves, and nearby vascular structures. For most of these situations, the bone can be replaced immediately with positive outcomes and limited complications. With more posterior tumors, however, a different approach may be needed. For instance, tumors in the posterior fossa, an area in the rear of the brain including the cerebellum and brainstem, a suboccipital or posterior fossa craniotomy would be indicated (Gnanalingham et al., 2002). In these situations, a bone window is made over the occipital lobe, which is then replaced after the procedure is complete.

Modern craniotomy is not entirely without risk of side effects, as it is still an invasive last-resort procedure. Among the most common complaints of those who survive their initial emergency are headaches, temporary weakness of the facial muscles, localized skin and muscle swelling, and bone resorption, or the breakdown of bone tissues by the body. Some may also experience leakage of the cerebrospinal fluid (CSF) or be at higher risk of

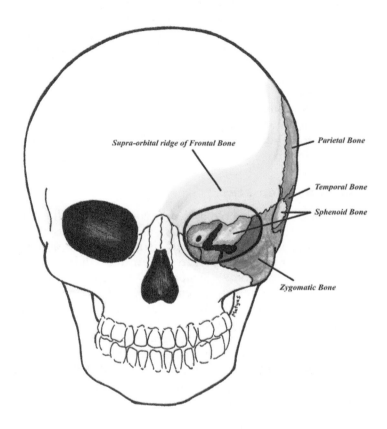

Figure 2.2 Location of the zygomatic arch and other bones of the skull of interest in an orbitozygomatic craniotomy. Exposure to the brain by this method allows access to the parasellar region, including the pituitary gland and vascular structures, among others.

infection. With the use of anti-inflammatory agents like steroids, intracranial swelling is not as severe as previously expected, and early cranioplasty can even reduce post-procedure side effects like headaches and CSF leakage (Gnanalingham et al., 2002; Faleiro et al., 2008). Many complications are found to be directly related to the particular approach taken, and can therefore be included in a contingency plan. Often, infections that occur after craniotomy may be treatable with antibiotics, but occasionally require another surgery to remove the offending abscess (Dashti et al., 2008). This is more often the case for surgeries intended to remove tumors and other masses than it is for vascular procedures, yet the occurrence rate is still low, with an estimate of less than 1 percent of total cranial surgeries being performed to remove infectious tissue that formed after craniotomy. Fortunately, with the care and caution used in surgeries targeting the brain or brain-adjacent structures, many live on with favorable outcomes and make significant recoveries.

Additional Remarks

If the idea of having a hole drilled in your head is still too creepy to imagine, remember that doing so is not a decision that is taken lightly. In certain situations, it may even be necessary to do a craniotomy while a person is alert and talking, referred to as an 'awake craniotomy' (Sahjpaul, 2000). Using local anesthetics and allowing a person to remain conscious allows us to map out the brain's major functions and areas of language dominance so that we do not remove too much, as in the case of temporal lobe epileptics undergoing scar removal. This is always done under the cautious hands of trained professionals who specialize in such techniques, and it is never recommended that craniotomy be performed by anyone other than skilled neurosurgeons. Nonetheless, that has not stopped a sub-set of the western population from practicing trephination for the purposes of enlightenment.

A small counter-culture group advocates for self-trephination, led by those who have successfully performed the procedure on themselves against the advice of medical professionals.[4] Theorizing that the adult brain requires a higher blood volume to operate at the cheerfully free level that young children's do, trephination advocates have attempted it to relieve depression, boost vitality, and even attain a permanent high (Colton, 1998; Doran, 2016). They report feelings of lightness and calm, as well as increases to metabolism and energy levels. These reports are most likely due to a sort of placebo effect, as those who do self-trephination expect to feel better afterwards and typically do, and the claims of the advocacy group are widely unfounded and unsupported. The dangers further outweigh any placebo effect, including infections like meningitis and direct damage to the brain itself (British Medical Journal 2000). The vast majority of doctors refuse to perform trephination on healthy adults, and none support the idea of doing it to oneself. Therefore, let the anthropological, neurological, and medical communities all reinforce the idea that you do *not* want to have a hole drilled in your skull unless it's absolutely necessary. And even then, please leave the procedure in the hands of a skilled surgeon.

Notes

1 Both spellings are correct in this case, as they are derived from a variety of Greek terms for a boring tool, or *trepanon*. Spellings may change according to the structure and functions of the instruments used for the procedure, but today they are widely accepted as synonyms.
2 There are numerous jokes about the use of cocaine in medical history, but prior to its surge as a recreational drug, derivatives of the coca plant were known to act reliably as an anesthetic and pain-reliever.
3 The living brain has about the consistency of gelatin, and will naturally shift to the top of the skull case when the head is placed in this position. This is particularly helpful, as we can use the extremely delicate nature of the brain to our advantage by letting it move out of our way on its own. For a fascinating video on how soft the human brain truly is, check out University of Utah's video 'The Unfixed Brain' online.
4 These individuals have made many public interviews, including Amanda Feilding, whose self-trephination was filmed and made into a documentary in 1970 by fellow trephination advocate Joe Mellen. The video, as well as some of their self-described details, are not for the faint of heart, and are not readily accessible to the public.

Chapter 3

'In with a Bang'

The American Crowbar Case, Mr. Phineas Gage

An Explosive Situation

If you ever took, are currently taking, or know someone who has taken a psychology class, chances are you've heard of Mr. Gage. Famously dubbed 'the American Crowbar Case', Phineas Gage was the American railway worker who, during a freak accident involving explosives, sustained severe brain damage and survived despite the odds being stacked against him. Even if the name does not sound familiar, the changes Gage experienced should: His personality showed drastic changes after the iron rod demolished his left frontal lobe. A formerly kind and well-liked man, Gage later became irritable and quick to anger, and his own friends claimed that this was no longer the same Phineas they knew before. These changes demonstrated to the fields of Psychology and Neuroscience that personality *must* be housed in the front-most portions of the brain. Why else would his personality have changed so much after such a specific type of injury?

There are some holes in the story as most people know it, starting with the title: The American Crowbar Case. No crowbar was involved in Gage's accident; however, other teams performing the same explosive procedure often used crowbars to tamp down the powder before igniting it. The shape of the crowbar made this difficult and imprecise. Gage sought a better method and commissioned a local blacksmith to make the custom iron he utilized, and which would later become famous. When retelling the story, though, other teams would not understand why the item was called a 'tamping iron' when everybody used crowbars, and so the name was altered for the sake of communication. Other holes in the story include a lack of evidence regarding just how outlandish his behaviors became, whether or not he became a 'vagrant', and his capability of holding onto employment.

The true story itself began on the worksite long before Occupational Safety and Health Administration (OSHA) regulations came into being. Prior to the incident, 25-year-old foreman Phineas Gage was a well-liked and intelligent man working in Cavendish, Vermont. He had even designed and engineered the method that his team was using to clear land for the railroad. This entailed boring a hole in the rock to be cleared, placing a carefully formulated mixture of explosives into the hole, covering the powder with sand as a protective barrier, and tamping it down (compacting the powder) with an iron rod (or crowbar) before introducing the spark to set off the explosive, preferably while the men were a good distance away. But something was not right on the day of the incident, September 13, 1848. A report by Dr. Bigelow, who met with and evaluated Gage after the incident, suggests that the sand barrier between the tamping iron and explosive powder was missing (Bigelow, 1850). According to Bigelow's report, Gage had ordered an assistant to place the sand barrier in place, but had turned his attention away and assumed the command had been fulfilled when it had not. He then began tamping the mixture down with his specially designed rod, and turned over his shoulder to talk to some of his coworkers (Figure 3.1).

Mistake number one: Distracted work is never good work. An errant spark, likely set off by the iron rod scraping against the rocks, ignited the explosive mixture while Gage was still holding onto the rod. Pressure built up rapidly below the rod, launching it like a bullet from its hole. While standing with his face still slightly turned to one side, the rod on its upward path passed under Gage's left cheek, behind his eye socket, and broke through the top of his skull. It then continued on its arc high into the air until finally landing on the ground some yards away from where it began. Gage was thrown onto his back and convulsed, but reportedly never lost consciousness.

The men working with Gage helped him to his feet and to a cart so they could get him to the nearest doctor. He was speaking ably and walked on his own along the path and even up a staircase with little assistance from his coworkers. John Harlow arrived over an hour later to find him covered in blood, occasionally vomiting more up, but otherwise calm, and hoping

Figure 3.1 Artist's suggestion for the posture Phineas Gage may have held at the time of the incident. His head was turned to one side, and his mouth was open, as he was speaking to a coworker when the explosive was set off.

the good doctor would tell him he was not too terribly hurt (Harlow, 1868; Neylan, 1999). Harlow joined an already present colleague, Dr. Williams, and began to clean and dress the man's wounds to determine the extent of the damage. Both men surely would have expressed some cynicism that the rod had indeed passed through the brain, as it was widely regarded at that time that such an injury would be immediately fatal. Local reverend Joseph Freeman even expressed his disbelief in writing, admitting that when told the bar had passed through Gage's head, he retorted, 'That is impossible'. However, the evidence now faced them and, coupled with several workmen's testimonies as to how the event happened, they readily acknowledged the 3½ inch round hole in Gage's cranium left by the rod, which was later found at the site of the accident with 'bits of blood and brain' still stuck to its surface. These claims were further supported when Dr. Bigelow later evaluated Gage, and gathered signed testimonies from those present on the day of the incident. Some even asserted that while vomiting, Gage appeared to be spitting up the same compounds that were also being discharged from his head, which was interpreted to be brain matter (about half a teacup full of brain fell out along with clotted blood, according to Dr. Williams). The wound was somewhat covered by three remaining fragments of bone, which the physicians removed so they could identify any other debris left in the injury site. As far as gaping wounds in the skull go, this one was apparently quite clean.

Imagine yourself placed in Dr. Harlow's shoes. It is 1848, and you are facing a large hole exposing a living man's brain. If your instinct would be to put your finger in that hole, (and admit it, you'd certainly be tempted to), then you are not alone. That is precisely what Dr. Harlow did. He also put another finger in the cheek hole, pointing them at each other as an attempt to line up the trajectory of the wound, with no resistance from either side. Keep in mind, Gage was conscious and alert through all of this. The idea of poking around in a person's body while they are awake to feel every pinch and prod would make most normal humans cringe, and is the basis of anesthesiology. Yet Harlow was actually criticized heavily for not introducing a full-length probe through the path of the wound, a decision he defended by citing that Gage's bleeding was only starting to subside, and further disruption of the tissue could prove dangerous or even fatal. But that one finger was just fine.

To dress Gage's wounds, the physicians kept things to routine, well-established methods. They cleaned the areas of debris, and bandaged and covered any openings. They replaced the larger bone fragments from his skull, a more recently established method based on findings that the bone was capable of fusing back together as it healed. His arms had also been burned in the explosion, and were cleaned and dressed accordingly. They put the man to bed with his head elevated and monitored him regularly. Much to our scientific fortune, Harlow kept excellent notes of Gage's progress and included them in his original publication of the case. A few hours after the initial wound dressing, Gage's bandages were soaked through, but the bleeding was at least slowing down. His friends asked after him, but he refused to see them, since he would be back at work in a few days anyway. The doctors asked if he could tell them who these friends were and where they lived, not unlike today's mini mental state exam (MMSE), a routine list of questions to determine whether the patient has awareness of their surroundings or has been experiencing confusion. He passed the test with flying colors.

By morning, Gage had stopped vomiting and his bleeding decreased to light seeping. Pain had set in, as had significant swelling of his face. He was still lucid, but did notice that vision in his left eye seemed compromised. This is not unexpected, as his eye was half protruded from the socket when he was brought in, likely pushed forward by the pressure of the rod as it passed behind the eye. By that evening, he had become somewhat agitated and delirious, and was given colchicum tincture to purge his system. While technically a poisonous plant, extracts from colchicum can induce diarrhea, and so it was one of many options doctors had to use as a laxative. Consider this era to be the Age of the Enema,[1] and it makes more sense as a routine treatment method. It was not particularly effective for Gage though, so the next day they added magnesium sulfate (commonly known as Epsom salts), which did its magic quite well.

The next morning, Gage's head wound started to show signs of infection. His face on the left side he self-reported as feeling 'banked up', a sensation that anyone who has had a severe sinus infection will surely empathize with. They applied ice water and cold compresses to his face and eye to relieve this. To add insult to injury, a fungal infection was beginning at the corner of his affected eye. Gradually over the next few days, his continuing rationale would fade into delirium, pocketed with lucid moments here and there, as the infection worsened and a fever set in. By September 22, nine days after the incident, Gage, and likely his doctors as well, did not expect to survive (his family had even prepared a coffin). They administered more laxatives, naturally.

Finally, there broke a light in the darkness, as Gage appeared more lucid the following morning. This was a short-lived spark though, as the fungal infection that began in his eye had begun to expand into the brain, and he entered a semi-coma like state. His left eye had lost all vision by now, and while he was awake and aware, he would only respond to others with monosyllabic answers. Silver nitrate[2] was applied to the infection, and the wound was debrided again. His infections, now multiple, were drained and kept clean, and eventually he began to show marked improvement.

Herein lies a personal favorite tale from his in-patient care: by October 5, about three weeks after the incident, Gage demanded his pants so he could get out of bed, even though he was not yet able to lift his head. He was able to roll to one side and rise to a seated position at the edge of the bed, though he only remained so for about four minutes. His infections were responding well to the silver nitrate treatments. Within another week, he was successful at getting up and about the room for a short amount of time, and was lucid once again. He could answer most basic questions, and was able to describe in accurate detail the event leading to his injury, as well as how long ago it had been. He recognized most of the people who asked after how he was doing, and his memory was completely intact. Harlow, however, estimated that Gage was unable to grasp size or money accurately anymore, as when offered a thousand dollars for a handful of pebbles from the riverbed, Gage adamantly refused. In about another week, Gage was up and walking readily, but rated as behaving in a childish way, expressing a desire to go home to New Hampshire. Another couple of weeks and he was walking about the house and outside, his injuries mostly healed closed by now. A short time later with few other major complications, Gage was able to leave the care of his physicians. Here is where Dr. Harlow's initial report ends.

A follow-up to Harlow's case was written two years later in 1850 by Professor Bigelow of Harvard University, who had convinced Gage to travel to Boston for another couple of months of observation after his wounds had healed closed (Bigelow, 1850). Harlow himself then further followed up on the case, but not until 1868, a full 20 years after the initial case, and 7 years after Gage had died from complications of seizure activity (Harlow, 1868). Within Harlow's follow-up, he cites that Gage returned to visit with him in the spring, and brought the fateful iron along with him. His wounds had fully closed by then, and signs of infection were gone, yet his eye was still lacking vision, and some of the bones of his cranium were out of place, either protruding where they ought not, or missing entirely, leading to the unusual ability to see the pulse of his heartbeat through his scalp. Gage was hoping to return to his previous job as foreman, though his employers reluctantly admitted that he had lost a bit too much to restore his position. There appeared to be a lack of 'balance' between his intellectual abilities and his impulsive, or 'animalistic', behaviors.

In plain English, it seemed that Gage was no longer acting quite like a rational adult, but would easily give in to rude or inappropriate behaviors, demonstrating a major lack of impulse control. Patterns appeared where those who knew him would state essentially that 'he wasn't like this before', for example regarding his use of vulgar language, his disregard for others' well-being, a loss of patience and flexibility, and trouble maintaining attention. The general consensus across those who knew him (besides his loving mother), was that Gage was 'no longer Gage'. This is quite a vague summary to end with, though, so many were left with more questions than they began with.

Bigelow's follow-up of the case differed from Harlow's mainly in his focus, intending to validate that the fantastic tale did indeed happen, and characterizing the physiology of Gage's recovery. He acquired signed testimonies of the original witnesses, and took a plaster cast of Gage's head to examine the changes to his skull's structure. Being quite thorough, Bigelow asserted that while some argued that maybe it was a fragment of stone that punctured Gage's head rather than the tamping rod, the stone had not been broken by the blast, and a stone could not have made such a clean transection of the head. Only a tapered solid structure, like iron, could have done that. In fact, had the stone theory been correct, it would have to have been a 1¼ inch sphere 'preceded by a conical and polished wedge', which to a modern reader sounds remarkably like a large bullet. To a modern scientist, it sounds even more like a non-sarcastic way of saying 'if it was a stone, it was a stone shaped like a giant bullet'.

Bigelow delved even deeper into the now-healed structures of Gage's face and scalp. By this time, January 1850, Gage's left eye was essentially fused closed and permanently swollen, all sight in it having been lost, and the muscles showing drooping. On his scalp, a chunk the size of an adult's palm appeared to have been raised partially like a hinge, which likely was pushed upward when the rod exited the skull. The 'hinged' portion of the bone would have been toward his forehead, with the top end of the bone being elevated near the coronal suture, or the point in the skull where the front and back fuse together, about at the very top of one's head. As an ever-vigilant scientist, Bigelow even sought replication of the case, and using a cadaver skull, drilled into it from the angle of the lower jaw upwards and through the top of the skull. This test left fractures remarkably similar to those reported in Gage's case, down to the incomplete damage done to the facial bones and the rear of the eye socket.

The recreation of the rod's trajectory suggested that the brain structures affected included the majority of the left frontal lobe, even laying open the lateral ventricle, one of the structures necessary for circulating cerebrospinal fluid. Based on the location of the exit wound, Bigelow suspected that a portion of the right hemisphere may also have been damaged. The optic nerve itself was left completely intact, though the damage to the eye socket and protrusion of the eye contributed more heavily to Gage's loss of vision, as the inflammation from his infections prevented it from returning to its proper place. Fortunately, the large opening in his skull provided an outlet for intracranial inflammation, so prolonged swelling in the brain was of less concern. Quite a relief, in fact, that if a large metal object was launched through your head, at least you wouldn't die of encephalitis.[3]

Aside from his Boston trip with Professor Bigelow, Gage visited most major New England cities, and stayed for a while in New York with P.T. Barnum, bringing his trusty iron rod with him as publicity (Figure 3.2).

This publicity tour itself was reported by those who knew Gage as very uncharacteristic of him, and may have been seen as another of the changes to his personality. He soon began working in stables with horses, later moving to Valparaiso, Chile, to do the same, until his health began to fail in late 1859. After

Figure 3.2 A daguerreotype portrait of Phineas Gage holding the iron rod that had pierced his brain, reprinted with permissions from the Warren Anatomical Museum in the Francis A. Countway Library of Medicine. The portrait was received by the museum as a donation from Jack and Beverly Wilgus.

rejoining his mother and sister in San Francisco and continuing his work with horses, Gage suffered multiple and increasingly frequent seizures, each of which would appear with no warning or sense of malaise beforehand (commonly called an aura). Early in the morning on May 21, 1861, he suffered a severe convulsion, and passed away later that evening, more than 12 years after the fateful injury that should otherwise have been fatal.

Follow-Up Findings

In textbooks, most attention is usually paid to Gage's personality changes (the swearing and irritability for example), and it did indeed go through significant changes, but not to the severity that folk lore suggests. One wild tale even suggests that Gage walked to the corner during a dinner party to urinate into a potted plant, though this story is unverified, and very likely unfounded. Modern studies claimed that Harlow had described Gage as a vagrant, unable to keep a job or remain in one place, which is yet again an unfounded claim. While Gage was not able to return to the job he had previously held, he was able to find new work and perform well at it. Harlow's report does state that Gage was childlike and obstinate (Harlow, 1868). He refused to do anything that was at odds with his desires, and loved to regale his nephews and nieces with fantastic tales of his own (fictitious) adventures. But let's be honest: Who among the aunts and uncles of the world has not told children wild tales for fun. Gage also grew fonder of animals than he had been, particularly horses and dogs, making his new living out of the former.

Among other documented changes that Harlow reported are an 'impatience of restraint', or a rise in impulsivity, a common outcome of damage to the orbitofrontal cortex (Torregrossa et al., 2008), fitfulness, decreases in empathy (described as irreverence toward others), and a tendency toward the fanciful, which he showed not only in the tales to his young family members, but also in forming numerous plans and projects that were quickly abandoned. The last of these symptoms may be characterized as a type of attentional disruption, as this rapidly changing thought pattern is common in individuals affected by attention deficits as well as certain dementias. As far as intact or unaffected functions, Harlow reported that Gage's gait and movement were strong and healthy, his speech as it always was, and his memory quite sharp. He could operate rather well in formal society, having walked to a shop and purchased items as normal, and he could still perform heavy work such as the care and livery of horses throughout the remainder of his life. When his health began to fail, he was cited as changing work often, though it is not clear if he had changed employers completely, or simply switched tasks when one became frustrating. This is once again where we enter the realm of conjecture, as it can be interpreted either as an inability to do the work or, more benignly, as a second manifestation of his irritability and quickness to frustration.

As Gage passed away among family and not under the care of his original physicians, history lost the advantage that an autopsy would have provided. However, Harlow later contacted Gage's mother, and with little effort convinced the family to exhume his remains and donate Gage's skull (and his iron) to the Museum of the Medical Department of Harvard University (Figure 3.3).

The exact brain regions damaged by the iron, therefore, were largely based on suppositions or experimental replications for many years after his death. More recently, imaging techniques and computer-generated images have provided a font of invaluable information in the field of neurotrauma, and several research teams sought to answer that long-unanswered question of what *exact* brain areas were damaged by the blast. Without the actual brain, we cannot give 100 percent certain answers, but we can get closer to the truth than we could before.

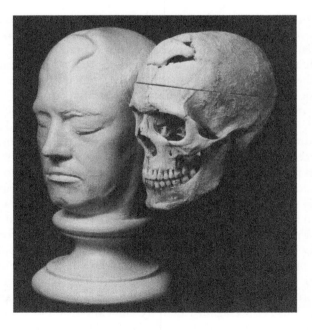

Figure 3.3 A life-mask cast of Phineas Gage not long after his fateful injury, shown next to his skull as displayed in a museum on the campus of Harvard College. This image is reprinted with permissions from the Warren Anatomical Museum in the Francis A. Countway Library of Medicine.

In trying to localize exactly where in the brain Gage's injury occurred, the case almost immediately hit resistance, as the accident took place during the fall of phrenology. Phrenology was a school of thought that sought to evaluate a person's psychological traits based on bumps and depressions in their skull and where they were located (Simpson, 2005). The idea of localization in the brain itself is today accepted, though the idea of using the skull to do so is now, and was then, laughable. Gall and Spurtzheim, the movement's founders, remained advocates of phrenology into the early nineteenth century, though at the time of Gage's accident, or perhaps even before this, the scientific community considered it to be complete pseudoscience. Like other more recent pseudosciences, phrenology remained an irritating sensitive spot for many practicing researchers, leading to some resistance on the idea of localization in neuroanatomy. Fortunately, Gage's case was able to separate the pseudoscience from reality and lend some credence to neural localization. Comparable suggestions were coming from research in France from Paul Broca, though these were still met with some resistance until experimental replication could be provided. The replication was shortly to follow with David Ferrier's experimental lesions in the monkey prefrontal cortex.

By the time of the Goulstonian lectures, Gage's case was well met with many others who had survived with an apparent absence of symptoms (Ferrier, 1878a). However, Ferrier narrowed this down to the absence of sensory-motor symptoms. Certainly, none of these cases resulted in paralysis, though to state that there were no recognizable effects would be a mistake. Following destruction of the prefrontal cortex, monkeys showed no impairments in their sensory faculties, which would be expected. However, their behaviors were decidedly changed. At first appearing to be less intelligent than the average monkey, these subjects now showed significant apathy and tendencies to drift off to sleep, and appeared to respond only in the moment and wandered back and forth without purpose. Essentially, they had grown impulsive and had difficulty maintaining attention. Importantly, Ferrier specified that they were *not* deprived of their intelligence, but of their attention and observational skills, a well-fitting match to Gage's symptoms.

Ferrier's criticisms of poor methodology with animal experimentation were certainly valid. We were limited at that time by our scientific capabilities. It would therefore be another century before imaging techniques were well developed enough to re-evaluate Gage. Damasio and colleagues in 1994 published findings from their evaluation of Gage's skull by x-ray photography (Damasio et al., 1994). Comparing the skull's structure and fracture locations to samples of healthy adult brains, five possible trajectories of the iron rod were suggested. One of these trajectories fit better than any other, indicating that the orbitofrontal cortex, medial frontal cortices, and anterior cingulate gyrus were all affected by the injury, as were connected white matter tracts. These areas are now well known to play significant roles in rational decision-making, as well as processing of emotion and regulation of behavior. However, while this was a well-done and laudable study, there is one factor that is not necessarily accounted for in their conclusion of bilateral frontal lobe damage: Gage's mouth was open at the time of the explosion.

Ten years after the x-ray photography study, Ratiu and colleagues expanded the search for the correct brain areas to include computed tomography (CT) scanning in evaluating Gage's skull, standardizing it to a 3D model of a healthy adult brain (Ratiu et al., 2004). Noting some particular cracks in the skull along the forehead and cheek, the opening beneath the cheek which appeared to be far smaller than the rod itself, and the missing molar in the jaw, this study then suggested a new trajectory. The tapered rod likely entered the cheek and passed through the sphenoid bone at the back of the eye, forcing the front portions of the skull to break and spread apart, closing back together once the rod had passed through. In plain English, it seems that Gage's skull broke open for the split second that the rod was occupying the space (Figure 3.4).

The broken flaps and hinges of the skull corroborate this suggestion, which further agrees with Harlow's original statement that the orbital socket was undamaged, as was the superior sagittal sinus, an area between the left and right hemispheres whose damage would have meant certain death at that time, and remains life-threatening today. Overall, Ratiu's findings indicate that Gage's injury was not bilateral, but was restricted to the left prefrontal lobe, and bypassed the optic nerve, superior sagittal sinus, and nearby major arteries.

Our curiosities about the brain we'll never see will never end, and many were left questioning how the relatively distant emotional center of the brain was so heavily affected in Gage when

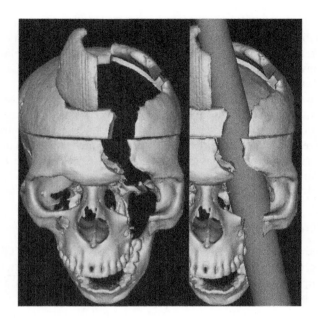

Figure 3.4 Reprint of Figure 3 from Ratiu and colleagues' 2004 reassessment of Phineas Gage's skull: Digital rendering of what may have happened to Gage's skull at the moment of impact as the rod passed through his head. In order to leave such a small entry wound in the ventral portion of the skull, and in concordance with the fracture lines observed on the anterior surface of the skull, Ratiu and colleagues suggest that portions of the skull separated laterally to allow the passage of the rod, then returned to their typical locations. In addition to accounting for Gage's mouth being open, this trajectory indicates that the direct damage was likely isolated to the left hemisphere. Image reprinted with permissions from Dr. Peter Ratiu.

his injury was specific to the left prefrontal lobe. As such, Van Horn and colleagues (2012) utilized a recently developed imaging technique to map white matter tracts: diffusion tensor imaging (DTI) (Van Horn et al., 2012). Using a CT scan of Gage's skull and inserting standardized imaging from 110 age and gender matched healthy volunteers, the research team was able to connect the acute damage to Gage's left frontal lobe to diffuse areas throughout the entire left hemisphere, as well as some areas in the contralateral right hemisphere. In particular, areas directly impacted by the loss of frontal lobe tissue include the left hemisphere's basal ganglia, insula, and limbic system, and the right hemisphere's frontal, insular, and limbic areas.[4] Damage to white matter projections from the orbital cortex and the basal forebrain especially would well explain Gage's behavioral effects. Artificial replication of the lesion showed additional support for these findings.

All follow-up experiments and imaging studies agree rather well with one another, with few exceptions, and conclude that based on these modeled trajectories and other clinical cases of frontal lobe damage, the orbitofrontal cortex most certainly plays a major role in the regulation of behaviors and emotions. Yet these are far from the only expectations we now have for individuals who are recovering from traumatic brain injury (TBI).

Lesser Known Effects of the Injury

While certain mental effects are now expected of frontal lobe TBI, such as increases in impulsivity, decreases in empathy, and attentional disruptions (Torregrossa et al., 2008), many individuals are blindsided by some of the lesser known effects. These do not happen to every individual with a frontal lobe TBI, but do occur frequently enough to warrant regular discussion in post-traumatic care and the planning of rehabilitation programs. Many of these effects will be discussed in greater detail in future chapters, and Gage was subjected to one in particular, which was ultimately responsible for his death: post-traumatic seizures.

Seizures. Classified by how quickly after the acute injury they occur, post-traumatic seizures (PTS) or post-traumatic epilepsy affects as few as 4 percent or as many as 53 percent of TBI survivors (Frey, 2003; Szaflarski et al., 2014; Ding et al., 2016). Risk factors that increase the likelihood of PTS developing include younger age, higher severity of the injury, and the presence of hemorrhage or residual metal within the brain. Children and combat veterans are at particularly high risk, and those who experience a single seizure will almost certainly have another within two years. PTS further increases in severity over time, and worsens the cognitive recovery of its victims. While it is unclear exactly when Gage began to experience his seizures, it is reported in Harlow's follow-up that after experiencing convulsions and failing health during his time in South America, his seizures began to worsen and grow in magnitude. The final cause of death was directly attributed to a particularly severe seizure that functionally shut down his body.

Currently, clinical medicine recognizes PTS as such a significant and common effect of TBI that a frequently recommended treatment option is prophylactic anticonvulsant medication (Szaflarski et al., 2014; Ding et al., 2016). This is heavily debated, as some classes of antiepileptics such as phenytoin may aggravate cognitive deficits. Other options include levetiracetam on a temporary basis, and if no seizure activity is detected within the first week post-injury, the medication is tapered off. These medications were not available during Gage's time of treatment, though interestingly, while magnesium sulfate in this case was administered to purge Gage's digestive tracts, it has some anti-convulsant effects, having been commonly used to address eclampsia convulsions in pregnant women (Sibai, 1990), and may have provided some added protection against the spasms that Gage was reported as showing.

Future Contributions

There is no doubt that Phineas Gage is the most famous case of head injury in psychology and neuroscience and shall remain the face of neurotrauma for years to come. Despite the injury occurring over 170 years ago, we are continuing to study and learn from him. Living individuals experiencing seizures or who are struggling with the cognitive and emotional effects of their injuries have benefited from Gage's case, however indirectly it may come about. Connecting his case to others and identifying matching features will build our knowledge base for as long as we remain curious, which will surely be never-ending.

Notes

1 Physicians often used laxatives and enemas to purge their patients' systems. While it may initially seem as senseless as bleeding to release 'bad blood', both clearly had to have had medicinal value, as some of these methods still survive today. Findings on gut flora and beneficial bacteria are being actively researched in regard to their relationship to brain health. If you wish to gross yourself out even more, I recommend reading about fecal transplants.

2 Another odd miracle cure was found in silver, having been used for centuries as a safe way to prevent bacterial growth. For some reason or another (there are many suggested rationales), silver is naturally

antiseptic, and is still used today in medical settings. Hypodermic needles made of silver seldom spread infection, and silver nitrate applied to the skin is an effective way to stop an existing infection in its tracks. It is also remarkably safe compared to other metallic compounds, with its most unusual side effect being the ability, particularly of colloidal silver taken in excess, to permanently turn people's skin blue. You can't make this stuff up.

3 Encephalitis refers to swelling of the brain. As discussed in the previous chapter, a historical treatment for this swelling was to simply provide an exit for the swollen tissue by drilling a hole in the skull. In Gage's case, his injury left a gaping hole anyway, so any swelling already had an exit. That's one way of saying if one door closes, a window (in the skull) opens.

4 Though based on Ratiu and colleagues' study, the right hemisphere was not directly damaged, die-back and atrophy are common after sustaining this level of trauma, particularly in white matter tracts.

Chapter 4

'No Words to Describe'

Patient Tan and Aphasias

Rendered Speechless

At around the same time as Phineas Gage was turning heads in the US, clinicians in France were arguing over localization, the concept that specific areas of the brain are responsible for specific roles. Many resisted the idea due to phrenology's pseudoscientific approach, but others were insistent that it was possible to determine the true locations of the brain's functions and map it out using scientific methods. Among these researchers were Bouillard, who asserted contralaterality, which refers to the tendency for the brain to control motor areas on the opposite side of the body to its brain area, and Aubertin, who was especially interested in cases that featured a loss of speech (Mohammed et al., 2018). A major leap forward came when a student of Bouillard's, Pierre Paul Broca, encountered a particular patient in Bicêtre Hospital with unusual symptoms. Nicknamed 'Patient Tan' by the staff due to his most prominent symptom, Monsieur Louis Leborgne was a long-time resident of the hospital who could not communicate verbally with staff, as he was unable to produce any speech other than the word '*tan*'.

A few patients had been observed before by Aubertin and Bouillaud, one of whom was only able to utter one unintelligible word followed by a profane outburst,[1] and each of whom presumably had some degree of damage done to the brain area responsible for articulated language (Broca, 1861). The precise area was yet to be determined, though autopsied cases had shown lesions in particular regions of the left frontal lobe. A major breakthrough came when Broca was sent to examine a long-term patient whose leg had become swollen and gangrenous, necessitating amputation.

Suffering from a progressively debilitating paralysis, Leborgne had entered the hospital 21 years prior when he had altogether lost his ability to speak. He maintained the ability to hear and understand others, and could use gestures for the most part to communicate his needs, but otherwise would only repeat the word *tan*, usually twice close together, and occasionally inserting an outburst of profanity when frustrated before reverting right back to his '*tan-tan*' speech pattern. Broca referred to this loss of speech but maintenance of comprehension and sanity as 'aphemia', a derivation of Greek terms for 'I speak; I pronounce'. Before his time in Bicêtre Hospital, Leborgne had been a lifelong epileptic who worked as a hat-form maker until age 30, when his speech was destroyed, though it is not clear if the loss was sudden or gradual before his admission. He was reported to have had a sour attitude, not getting along well with other patients or staff, and as time went on, lost more and more function on the right side of his body. By the time Broca had been sent to treat his inflamed leg, he had lost the use and much sensation of his right arm, right leg, and a significant portion of his vision starting in the left eye. Broca called Aubertin to examine Leborgne further, and they agreed that the man's issue had to have begun in the left frontal lobe based on his progression of symptoms, and that it must have been a slow, progressive softening of the tissue rather than the presence of a tumor. Leborgne passed away nearly a week after Broca's initial examination of him, and his brain was collected at autopsy and preserved.

It was immediately apparent that Leborgne's brain was severely damaged. The meninges were thickened and filled with fluid, areas of it appeared infected, and the entire brain had atrophied to varying degrees (Broca, 1861). Nothing within the brain appeared to be completely healthy, though most notable was a lesion in the left hemisphere just above the Sylvian fissure, which separates the temporal lobes from the frontal lobes, about the size and depth of an egg with softening of tissue in the surrounding areas. Broca particularly highlighted that the focal point of the lesion was within the third convolution (or gyrus) of the frontal lobe, which was clearly the starting point of Leborgne's symptoms (Figure 4.1).

The deeper striatum structure was somewhat softened, but otherwise intact, and the overall brain had lost about a quarter of its volume compared to healthy age-matched brains. While there

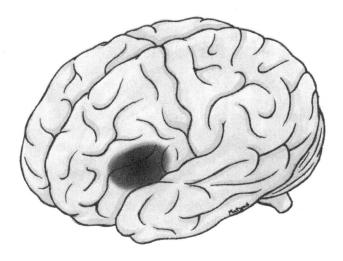

Figure 4.1 Approximate size and location of the focal point of Louis Leborgne's speech-impeding lesion. This region has since been known as Broca's area in deference to the skilled physician who identified it. This focal point was far from the only region that showed damage and degeneration in Leborgne's brain, but was likely the initial insult that contributed to his loss of speech.

could be no doubt that Leborgne had widespread symptoms, the progression of his paralysis and the evidence that his lesions had begun in the left frontal lobe suggested that this focal point Broca identified must be the home of speech within the brain.

Broca's original publication on the speech center of the brain did not receive a large amount of attention at first, instead receiving criticism that there existed other cases of left hemisphere damage in which there were no apparent aphemia symptoms. He later defended this claim, not by denying the existence of such patients, but emphasizing that these patients appeared to be largely left-handed, reducing the likelihood that their left hemisphere was the 'dominant hemisphere' for language, and providing evidence for a sort of internal back-up system in those whose brains are not arranged in the typical, left-specific orientation (Ferrier, 1878b; Broca, 2011). These exceptions could also be apparent in other health conditions, such as in a child born without the use of the right hand, and who becomes readily capable with the left hand. This child would therefore have a more richly developed right hemisphere instead, and the speech center may be shifted or reorganized to coincide with this increase in detailed motor skills. Such theories and early results in trying to re-teach speech-deprived patients how to speak indicated that, like a child learning to write with their left hand, a person who has lost their speech can re-train their brain to speak again using the intact right hemisphere. While today's knowledge of speech therapy and rehabilitation are quite different, Broca was ahead of his time in regard to this, particularly in his suggestions that younger patients fared better than older, and that longer, more intensive therapy sessions would lead to more significant progress in speech recovery.

Once his findings were made known to the larger scientific community, Broca's term of 'aphemia' was adapted to the now-common 'aphasia', meaning a loss of language or speech, and others began to explore the details of the suggested speech center within the brain. General consensus regarding Leborgne's brain, based on initial examination as well as Broca's report, states that Leborgne likely suffered an ischemic stroke, or blockage of the blood vessels that feed the brain, starving it of oxygen and nutrients and thereby killing the brain area that would otherwise have been maintained by that blood vessel (Broca, 1861; Mohammed et al., 2018). This suggestion has been repeatedly supported by other stroke victims who sustained damage to the perisylvian region and experienced some degree of aphasia immediately afterward. In honor of its discoverer, this region is now referred to as Broca's area, and the behavioral effects of deficits in speech production is called Broca's aphasia or non-fluent aphasia, the latter of which emphasizes the broken rhythms in speech of those affected. Current theories on the functions of Broca's area suggest that the region is more involved in coordination and processing of information prior to the production of speech by the motor cortex.

Despite having the region named after him later on, Broca tried to be clear that the language center was not a clearly defined area delineated by the convolutions of the cortex, and that the region was more likely to have a fuzzy boundary area around it. It was a position shared by anatomist Korbinian Brodmann, who mapped out the human cortex slide by slide based on detailed cell-staining techniques (Zilles & Amunts, 2010). Brodmann's map was so carefully collected and compared to the brains of other non-human primates that it is still widely used today, redefining Broca's area under anatomical terminology as Brodmann's Area 44. The map was later broken down even further into a modern interpretation known as Ojemann's mosaic, in which small electrical stimulations on the surface of the brain area are carried out to determine which specific zones interrupt speech while an alert patient participates in active object-naming tests (Ojemann et al., 1989). The Ojemann's mosaic model of speech anatomy within the brain allows for small variations between individuals, and may even be useful as a pre-surgical tool to minimize the risk of aphasia after necessary resection procedures.[2]

In light of changes to the way we approach brain anatomy and mapping, multiple studies have attempted to revisit the original case of Leborgne's pervasive aphasia. Because Broca had been thorough enough to preserve his patients' brains, modern technology could be utilized to collect detailed information that would have otherwise been impossible during the nineteenth century. In 2007, magnetic resonance imaging (MRI) was used on both Leborgne's preserved brain and that of a similar patient known as Lelong, whose speech was limited to a collection of five words: the French words for yes, no, three, always, and a shortened version of his own name (Dronkers et al., 2007). While Broca's assessment of Leborgne's brain described a devastating lesion, MRI scans showed that it was even more severe than previously estimated, extending into the basal ganglia deep within the brain, and destroying the entire insular cortex. Areas of the medial parietal lobe were compromised, as were several white matter tracts between regions. Lelong fared better, though his brain still showed significant damage and atrophy not only in Broca's area, but also the insula, with smaller pockets of damage to the superior longitudinal fasciculus. The white matter tracts damaged in each brain are now known to play active roles in language processing, and may explain why these two men did not recover their speech abilities, as many modern patients do over time. Other approaches have emphasized these behavioral differences in aphasia, suggesting that under the scope of modern speech and language pathology studies, Leborgne may not have had true Broca's aphasia, but a more pervasive global aphasia (Selnes & Hillis, 2000).

Wernicke and Other Aphasias

Leborgne and Broca's other aphasic patients were far from the only examples of speech disturbances known to history. In Russia, the Bolshevik leader Vladimir Lenin experienced progressive cardiovascular disease, which gradually rendered him speechless (Teive et al., 2011). As his disease progressed, he struggled to communicate and eventually was only able to respond to questions with the phrase 'vot-vot'. Similarly, the French poet Baudelaire suffered cardiovascular disease, further complicated by neurologically active syphilis, which led to his speech being limited to repetitions of 'cre-nom', an abbreviated form of the profanity seen in other cases of aphasia. Yet these still consist of situations where the individual maintained their understanding of language; only their speech seemed to be heavily affected. Aubertin had attempted to explain this by positing that there were separate brain structures dedicated to pronunciation, movements of the face and mouth, and communication between these regions (Lorch, 2011). Surely enough, cases of aphasia were soon found that featured no apparent damage to the proposed speech center of the brain, indicating the existence of other regions that contribute to language.

Following Meynert's discovery of the auditory nerve's connections into the cortex, Carl Wernicke began exploring the temporal lobe for an area that controlled reception of speech (Lanczik & Keil, 1991). His work differentiated Broca's motor aphasia from sensory aphasia, which was later to be called Wernicke's aphasia or fluent aphasia. In contrast to Broca's aphasia, individuals with Wernicke's aphasia can speak fluidly with appropriate inflections. The problem instead lies in the content of speech, which may be nonsensical or random, an artifact known as word salad, which also appears in schizophrenia. Rather than affecting a person's ability to speak, Wernicke's aphasia often involves being unable to comprehend language.

As the field of speech and language pathology developed, more specific variations of both Wernicke's and Broca's aphasias were identified. The pure forms of either are subjectively rare, as most natural cases of aphasia will not be isolated to a single brain region, much in the way that Leborgne's lesion spread far outside of Broca's area (Figure 4.2).

As in the suggestion that Leborgne had a more extensive type of aphasia than Broca's aphasia, global aphasia is considered to be the most severe form of aphasia, and applies to individuals who struggle with recognition of language as well as reading and writing, and tends to persist for significantly longer times than other forms of aphasia (NAA, 2020). On Wernicke's side of the speech pathology spectrum, anomic aphasia describes an inability to find the words one would like to use, though comprehension may be spared. Yet another sub-type of aphasia is Primary Progressive

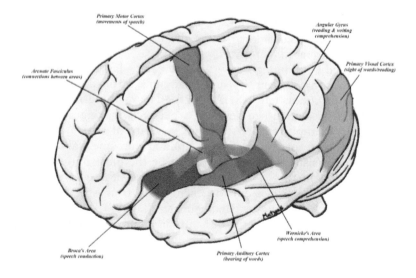

Figure 4.2 Estimation of the brain areas involved in the modern Wernicke-Geschwind model of speech and language, including Broca's area for speech production, Wernicke's area for speech comprehension, the arcuate fasciculus that connects these two regions, the angular gyrus for reading and writing comprehension, and primary sensory and motor cortices involved in each corresponding aspect of language.

Aphasia, in which speech is gradually deteriorated by some form of disease or degeneration, such as Alzheimer's disease or cardio-vascular dementia.

As seen in many of the historical cases of aphasia, cardiovascular disease may lead to repetitive ischemic events or strokes which damage small regions of the brain. Transient Ischemic Attacks (TIAs) may even go unnoticed and therefore undiagnosed, and these small pockets of damage build up over time, leading to progressive damage such as that seen in Primary Progressive Aphasia. As such, a large portion of individuals who seek therapy for aphasias have survived one or more strokes. Among the most common types of aphasia observed after a single stroke, global aphasia was the most common at onset, followed by anomic, Wernicke's, Broca's, and other forms (Pedersen et al., 2004). To the fortune of many patients, this tends to change over time, and within a year of onset, the majority of patients saw their aphasias shift to a less severe form. It is therefore recommended that therapists not announce an overly pessimistic outcome for clients, seeing that global aphasics, considered to be the most severe, often benefit greatly from speech therapy.

Prior to beginning any speech and language therapy, a thorough assessment by a trained and certified professional needs to be conducted (ASHA, 2020). This will aid in determining the particular difficulties that a person is having and design a custom therapy regimen to begin. Severity of stroke has good reliability in regard to predicting aphasia outcomes, as does the type of aphasia. Prognosis appears to be the most optimistic for individuals with Broca's aphasia in terms of degree of recovery, while global aphasics seem to benefit more from speech therapy than Wernicke's aphasics (Bakheit et al., 2007). One potential explanation for this was the difficulty in comprehension for those with Wernicke's aphasia, as those with other forms of aphasia may have less difficulty understanding instructions and following through with therapy regimens. Symptoms may persist throughout life, though with a customized speech therapy program, most can recover at least some of their language abilities.

Future Research

Broca may not have had as much attention at the time of Leborgne's case as he does today, though none can deny that his discovery helped to pioneer the relatively young field of speech and language pathology. Far from the attitude of general neglect given to Leborgne during his time in Bicêtre, we now recognize that many victims of aphasia are still able to think and understand as they did before their onset of illness, and people are given the time and respect deserved to them. It is important not to assume that because a person is unable to speak clearly, they do not comprehend speech either. Diagnoses of aphasia should, of course, be left to trained professionals, who can develop personalized plans for functional recovery. The promotion of such programs as well as prevention of cardiovascular disease can hopefully indicate that, in the future, those who are rendered speechless are only subjected to it temporarily.

Notes

1 The use of profanity is a common trend in historical aphasia cases, and in studies on the use of swearing, profanity appears to be more of an emotional artifact than a language artifact. For more information on why profanity is a common and perhaps even necessary part of human life, see Emma Byrne's book *Swearing is Good for You.*
2 Another pre-surgical test is the WADA test, in which sodium amytal is injected into the carotid arteries to numb one hemisphere of the brain at a time and identify which hemisphere is responsible for speech and language and for memory. It is often done prior to focal resections in epileptic patients whose seizures do not respond to typical medications.

Chapter 5

'We're All Mad Here'

Mercury Toxicity and the Origin of the Phrase 'Mad as a Hatter'

Occupational Hazards

Inspiring dozens of films and television specials, Lewis Carroll's timeless novels *Alice's Adventures in Wonderland* and *Through the Looking Glass* and the memorable characters within are now a staple of popular culture (Figure 5.1).

Several of these characters stand out as icons of the stories, though few are as strongly associated with the scattered insanity of Wonderland as the Mad Hatter. The mentally unstable artisan with unorganized speech and what many suggest is some sort of psychosis (or 'madness') only adds to Alice's confusion, telling her that she is 'entirely bonkers', yet 'all the best people are'. In the modern day this line is used as a reminder that mental illness affects everyone, and is as encouraging as Carroll's Hatter likely intended. But why was he really called 'mad' in the first place? Surely his unorganized mind was an indication, but we are never told precisely what made him that way in the first place.

While only Carroll can say for sure why the ubiquitous Hatter was the way he was, it's been often suggested that the key to the character's mind lies in his occupation as a hatter. Indeed, the phrase 'mad as a hatter' was already a mainstay in British culture before the story's publication, as the occupation was strongly connected to a specific pattern of mental illness. Hatters often developed physical symptoms such as general malaise, gait disruptions like lurching steps, and respiratory illnesses (Lee, 1968), as well as hallucinations, speech disruptions, tremors (nicknamed 'hatters' shakes'), and became emotionally unstable (Nix, 2018; Corrosion Doctors 2019b). In the US, it was further nicknamed 'the Danbury Shakes', after the nineteenth century fashion capital

Figure 5.1 Artist's illustration merging two of Lewis Carroll's classic characters, the Cheshire Cat and the Mad Hatter. Fans and historians speculate that the titular 'mad' hatter character may have been based on the common finding that skilled artisans exposed to neurotoxic mercury often showed signs and symptoms of psychological illness.

of Danbury, Connecticut. Danbury hatters reported also having excess drooling, hair loss, and confusion on top of the previously listed symptoms. Not every hatter was subjected to the syndrome, of course, but it was widely recognized as an occupational hazard as early as the late nineteenth century, eventually being placed under stricter health and safety regulations in the mid-twentieth century (Lee, 1968; OSHA, 1970).

As to why hatters specifically were affected by this unusual cocktail of symptoms, the answer lies in a chemical process used to separate fur from pelts to form the felt used in high-end head ware. Called 'carrotting' because of the vibrant orange color of the chemicals, wet felting soaked pelts in warm solutions containing mercury nitrate to loosen the hairs and encourage them to mat together smoothly into a solid piece of workable fabric, which would then be heated in an oven to dry it (Von Delpech, 1874; Van den Broeck, 2018). The heat of the oven would then release mercury vapors into the air, which workers inevitably inhaled, compounding their exposure after already having immersed their hands in the toxic solutions. Some opted to paint the solution onto the pelts rather than immersing it completely, though the issue of heat-released vapors was still a present danger. Eventually, alternatives to mercury were established, such as molasses (Von Delpech, 1874) and a diluted mixture of nitric and hydrochloric acids (Dargelos, 1888).

But why mercury in the first place? A rumor passed down through the industry claims that based on the traditional use of camel urine to work with straight, coarse hairs,[1] Frenchmen started using their own urine, and that of one particular hatter produced an especially high-quality felt (Van den Broeck, 2018; Corrosion Doctors, 2019). Once it was discovered that the man was being treated with mercury for syphilis, the artisans switched to mercury nitrate. Recognition of the hazards was met with the argument of *volenti non fit injuria*, or the claim that men who choose to do dangerous work do so voluntarily in acknowledgement of the dangers (Lee, 1968). This fits with some of the film versions of the Mad Hatter, as the character takes great pride in the quality of his hats. To a true artist, the craft is worth any pain it takes to create it.

Hats would, of course, fall out of fashion in the early twentieth century, as most trends inevitably do, and with it fell the frequency of mercury poisonings. Today, the most significant concern for mercury exposure is environmental, primarily through the consumption of fish and the creation of metallic amalgams (Carvalho et al., 2008). Other mercury-containing compounds are overall safe, and regulations have recognized for decades that certain compositions of mercury can lead to high levels in excretion without any symptoms of poisoning (Lee, 1968). This includes still-used preservatives such as thimerosal, commonly included in vaccines, which was briefly explored as a potential factor in the development of autism, but which has also since been widely debunked and found to be harmless (Stehr-Green et al., 2003). To date, the only connection between vaccines and autism is the coincidence that children's booster shots tend to take place at the same age at which patterns of autism begin to appear. Therefore, the dangers of the diseases prevented by vaccines are dramatically higher than the minimal risk of adverse vaccine reactions. In terms of mercury exposure, the consumption of fish is deemed to be far more dangerous than vaccines, and even then is marginal compared to industrial exposure.

Mechanisms of Toxicity

While mercury poisoning never quite reached epidemic levels, the scientific community nonetheless sought to establish what the chemical actively does to the brain that creates the issues seen in Victorian-era hatters. Understanding how mercury damages tissues can help us prevent similar issues in the future and confirm the safety of medicinally effective compounds like thimerosal. Mercury compounds have traditionally been used in medical treatments for syphilis and skin conditions,[2] sparking exploration of organic versus inorganic forms (Friberg, 1991; Carvalho et al., 2008). As with any other chemical structures (solid-state sodium is highly explosive, chlorine gas is immediately toxic, but the two added together into a stable salt is constantly added to most foods that humans consume), mercury behaves differently in different structures. Mercury itself inhibits enzymatic reactions and production of proteins, and similarly to other metals, affects the electrical conduction of nerves (Aschner & Aschner, 1990). The organic form, methylmercury, is especially hazardous, found primarily in glial cells such as astrocytes once passing through the blood-brain barrier. Unsurprisingly, chronic exposure has more significant effects than acute exposure, explaining the differences in symptoms between hatters and those who were exposed only in isolated accidents or situations. More recent work has explored the thioredoxin system, which interacts readily with methylmercury, inhibiting growth and contributing to cytotoxicity, or cell death (Carvalho et al., 2008). The thioredoxin system is known to influence inflammation and cell adhesion, and its activity is reduced when bound to mercury compounds. This also highlights the differences between the organic and inorganic forms, in which inorganic mercury chloride has stronger effects than organic methylmercury, though both present dangers to the CNS as well as physical health. The level of exposure required for such activity of course affects how dramatically the system is inhibited, and an individual's existing health, diet, and susceptibility will also change the way mercury binds within the body.

Future Research

While we cannot say for certain that Lewis Carroll was basing his beloved characters off of mercury-poisoned craftsmen, we do know that real-life hatters were often exposed to neuro-toxic mercury. Alternative techniques are now available, and even though most people no longer wear felt top hats, the recreation of historical styles is a living art form, and modern artisans can follow the old protocol without risk of mercury exposure. Current exposure to mercury is relatively isolated to dietary sources and medical interventions, the latter of which is heavily regulated and controlled. The vaccine preservative thimerosal has been identified as a safe, non-toxic compound, yet research is actively exploring alternatives so that any min-imal risk may be completely eliminated. Dietary sources, on the other hand, are more difficult to regulate. Doctors often recommend that women of childbearing age limit fish con-sumption because of mercury's effects on development, though the type of fish and where it is caught may alter the amount of mercury consumed. In general, awareness and exposure-prevention have all but eradicated occupational mercury poi-soning. The next step is to do the same for environmental and dietary risks.

Notes

1 Camel urine produced the best quality felts, but why urine made it into the mix in the first place is unclear.
2 Aside from treating skin infections, mercury has also been used as a skin lightener in cosmetics.

Chapter 6

'My World of Pure Imagination'

Roald Dahl's Journey from Fighter Pilot to Children's Author

Emergency Crash Landing

At the outbreak of World War II in Europe, hundreds of thousands of young people were spurred to enlist, driven to protect their families, homes, and countries. Among these people was a tall, slender young Englishman of Norwegian descent. Then working in Tanganyika in eastern Africa, Roald Dahl was vocal about his opposition to the Germans' actions, even being reprimanded by supervisors for openly throwing darts at a naked drawing of Adolf Hitler while surrounded by German Nationalist coworkers (Sturrock, 2010). While characteristic of his bold and stubborn personality, Dahl would soon find himself in an exaggerated form of himself, which he would later describe as one of the reasons for his success as a children's writer.

Dahl enlisted as a special constable at the start of the war, but disgusted by the general pattern of human behavior in the army encampments, soon signed on with the Royal Air Force, passing his condensed training with high marks (Sturrock, 2010). On September 19, 1940, he climbed into his Gloster Gladiator plane and headed to the North African desert to meet his squadron. However, the sun was beginning to set, darkness was setting in, and Dahl had never been to the undisclosed camp location before. He decided it would be safest to make an emergency landing until sunrise, then wait to be found. On lowering altitude, a boulder struck the undercarriage of the Gladiator and threw the aircraft into the ground where it burst into flames. Dahl's face smashed into the front of the canopy, fracturing his skull and nose, and knocking him unconscious. He awoke to the smell of gasoline, but found he could not open his eyes, for they were swollen shut (and would remain so for weeks after the crash). Tempted to just go to sleep and let the flames have him, Dahl managed to free himself from the wreckage and roll to extinguish the fire on his clothing. Though he did not remember (or at least discuss it openly), there was another officer there that night, who stayed with Dahl through the night until help could arrive.

Diagnosed with a severe concussion among his other injuries, Dahl recovered quickly, even resisting orders to return to England to rest because he might potentially return to flying once again. He fought through what would now be called post-concussive syndrome, characterized by memory troubles, irritability, disrupted concentration, and severe headaches, had his crushed nose reconstructed, and returned to war, surviving multiple battles and witnessing constant death and destruction. Though not mentally ready for discharge, Dahl was relieved of duty when his constant, severe headaches progressed into blackouts and made him unable to safely fly and navigate his plane. He was subsequently transferred into a position as an air attaché in the US, soon finding a knack for writing and publishing outlandish short stories, first in the genre of adult fiction, and later on in his most famous genre of children's novels.

Based on descriptions in his official biography, the personalities and behaviors of Dahl as well as his immediate family might lead some to suggest his injury did not have too much of an effect on his mental status. He was bold and eccentric as a young man, and remained such for long after the plane crash. However, the author himself described his own changes as a major contributor to his success as an author, claiming that it had 'materially altered his personality and inclined him to creative writing' (Sturrock, 2010). Any sense of feeling embarrassed was minimal if not non-existent, his imaginative sense of fantasy was magnified, and he harbored an intense desire to shock people with surprising and appalling stories. He considered it to be Sudden Artistic Output Syndrome, wherein the 'monumental bash on the head' unleashed a hidden talent that had been buried deep within his brain (Johnson, 2016). A physician who knew him later in life, Dr. Solomon, agreed that this frontal lobe damage would certainly have tipped the scales for Dahl and pushed him deeper into the world of fantasy and disinhibited flow of ideas. He would write about his crash to some degree in multiple stories, including fictionalized pieces

'Shot Down Over Libya' and 'Beware of the Dog', and later on more honest descriptions in 'Lucky Break' and *Going Solo* (Howard, 2016).

Aside from his own injuries, Dahl's family experienced more than their fair share of neurotrauma cases, each of which would be deserving of its own individual discussion. At four months old, his son Theo was struck by a taxi and thrown against the side of a bus, crushing his skull. While he recovered amazingly well in the end, the trauma led to chronic hydrocephalus, a buildup of fluid within the brain, for which Dahl got involved in developing a shunt[1] to treat it that was highly resistant to blockages (Sturrock, 2010; Solomon, 2016). His wife, Pat, then suffered a severe stroke due to a ruptured aneurism, after which he helped write and standardize intensive rehabilitation therapy techniques. Soon afterwards, their eldest daughter, Olivia, developed encephalitis due to measles complications and died, prompting a heartfelt letter years later in support of the vaccine that was developed too late to have saved her (Dahl, 1986). The letter is still being recirculated today in opposition to a surge in anti-vaccination debates to prompt parents to do what is best to protect their children. Finally, his step-daughter, Lorina, passed away suddenly from an aggressive and undiagnosed brain tumor. Dahl himself survived all of the complications of his original injury, though not without struggling along the way, ultimately passing away from myelofibrosis, a rare sub-type of leukemia.

Lifelong Residual Effects

According to Dahl's own self-reports, he did not suffer much from the psychological changes that his injury appeared to cause. In this regard, it may be considered a 'disorder of the observer', in which the individual is not as bothered by their symptoms as those they interact with. What did bother Dahl, on the other hand, was his most prominent physical symptom, and one that is extremely common in others with traumatic brain and spinal cord injuries: pain. Severe headaches resulted in his being removed from active duty during the war, and the pain in his back became a recurring problem, necessitating at least six surgeries over the course of his life. Letters to and from his family, as well as comparisons with others affected by similar types of pain, highlight just how serious this pain must have been.

Psychological Changes. Considering both the self-reported and observer-reported symptoms that Dahl regularly portrayed brings to mind the impulsiveness of Phineas Gage. However, where the eccentric behaviors reported about Gage are largely unfounded, Dahl's wild tales are well supported. Aside from describing himself as having lost his sense of embarrassment, Dahl's youngest daughter, Lucy, cited that it was impossible for him to keep any secrets, and that he loved to gossip (Sturrock, 2010). He criticized people who seemed to him to be closed-minded, and frequently would host dinner parties that ended in screaming arguments, once even ending dinner in the middle of dessert and asking everyone to leave. He thrived on annoying others, finding it to be far more entertaining than calmness. At times, his mother also described him as tiring easily, requiring more rest than others, and potentially explaining his quickness to frustration. To those who grew up reading his wild tales of adventures, though, these traits truly did form him into a household name.

Post-Traumatic Headaches. Now included in the list of symptoms for post-concussive syndrome, headaches are among the most common side effect of TBIs, affecting as much as 95 percent of those with concussions, comparatively the mildest individual[2] form of TBI (AMF, 2018). Symptoms may be similar to common migraines, or may take on other features, such as those of cluster headaches, and tend to get worse over time. Dahl described his own as 'like having a knife driven into your forehead' (Sturrock, 2010). Unlike seizures, post-traumatic headaches (PTH) show no relationship between the severity of the TBI and the magnitude of the headache (Hoffman et al., 2011), and often are more common in milder cases of TBI (Mayer et al., 2013). Individuals in military service are at particularly high risk for PTH, as stress and PTSD can aggravate the condition.

Treatments for PTH most often address the features of the headache. For instance, a migraine-like headache will be treated with medication that targets common sources of migraine. Pathology, though, differs between naturally occurring migraine disorders and PTH. Increased inflammation and diffuse damage in TBI have been identified in PTH, which is not present in pre-existing migraine disorders. Maladaptive activity in the trigeminal nerve that feeds the side of the head and face may also contribute to PTH (Mayer et al., 2013), as may structural changes to the orbitofrontal areas of the brain

(Schwedt et al., 2017). This therefore indicates that we may need to shift the target of PTH treatment methods to better improve the lives of those affected.

Spinal Degeneration and Pain. Though blinding headaches are cited as the main reason Dahl was relieved of active duty, the back pain that developed after the plane crash was arguably worse. The exact nature of his back pain is unclear, though his symptoms and surgical history (numbness in the fingers and multiple laminectomies and discectomies) suggest damage and degeneration of the intervertebral discs, as well as pinching and/or crushing of the spinal root nerves.

In a healthy spine, the vertebral bones are separated from one another by the intervertebral discs, sponge-like structures composed of collagen, proteoglycans, and water, and which act as shock absorbers and assist with bending and rotational movements (Matyas, 2012). The spinal cord runs through the column behind these discs, putting out roots at gaps between the bones (Figure 6.1).

Degeneration of these discs is startlingly common, being identified in more than 90 percent of individuals over the age of 60, though only a small percentage of those lead to specific medical complaints. Problematic degeneration types can include calcification of the cartilage endplate, dehydration and loss of mobility, and prolapse of the central pulposus structure. The latter of these issues, if it takes place in the wrong location of the disc, can compress the spinal nerve root, leading to severe pain or numbness, and in extreme cases, paralysis. In Roald Dahl's case, numbness in the hands indicates that there may have been a disc prolapse in the cervical spine, which runs from the base of the skull to the bottom of the neck. The prominent current treatment for this is still to remove the offending prolapse, or in situations like Dahl's, remove the entire disc itself and supporting the spine's structure with hardware implants. However, this was largely unsuccessful in reducing his pain, and for many others, spinal fusion with hardware can actually worsen the condition by spreading degeneration to adjacent spinal columns (Ganey & Meisel, 2002).

Recommended specialists for treating intervertebral disc issues include orthopedists, osteopaths, and neurologists, depending on the source of the issue (including joint, bone, or nerve problems). In an orthopedic attempt at treatments, Dahl wore a brace to strengthen

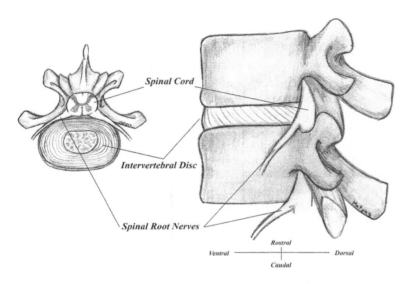

Figure 6.1 General anatomy of a spinal segment, featuring the bony processes, intervertebral disc, and spinal root nerves. Dahl's persistent back pain and numerous surgeries may have involved a number of these structures, including degeneration and/or prolapse of the intervertebral disc, compression of the spinal root nerves, and laminectomy or removal of the dorsal bony processes of the spine.

his spine, the main theory being that artificially raising the height of the spinal discs would slow or impede the degeneration process. By 1967, however, his pain had spread, and by 1980, he had gone through six spinal operations. He had also lost two inches of height by this time, an almost certain sign that multiple spinal discs had degenerated and/or collapsed. Modern studies are integrating the use of adult-source stem cells, including those obtained from fat, known as adipose tissue. Having been successfully tested in dogs with degenerative disc disease, adipose-derived stem cells are particularly helpful for the treatment of degenerating joints, and can be obtained from one's own body, eliminating the risk of immune rejection (Ganey et al., 2009). Another exciting new technology, 3D-printing scaffolds and structures to artificially replace the damaged disc, may be engineered to absorb and grow one's existing cells and tissues *in vitro* (Rosenzweig et al., 2015). With these and other new advancements, the pain and numbness that Roald Dahl suffered for decades will hopefully be an artifact of the past.

Additional Remarks

The story of Roald Dahl, like those he wrote for so many children, is a fascinating one. And while many likely read his biography to learn of the unique and eccentric behaviors he showed after sustaining a head injury during the war, we cannot exclude the pain he endured as well. For over 40 years, the treatments he received failed to completely eliminate his pain, though they were the best available procedures of the time, and many still remain viable options for people today. Identifying the source of pain, whether bound to the head or radiating through the back and limbs, is key to forming an appropriate treatment plan, which as with any other case, should be catered specifically to the individual. With progress and communication, we can therefore look forward to a day when there will no longer be a need for repetitive and ineffective procedures.

Notes

1 The shunt was patented as the Wade-Dahl-Till valve, named for its contributors.
2 Individual form, in this case, refers to a single isolated incident. Compound injuries, or repeated concussions/TBIs, will be discussed in depth in a later chapter in the context of chronic traumatic encephalopathy.

Chapter 7

'Fast, Affordable Brain Surgery for Everyone!'

Walter Freeman, Pioneer of the Transorbital Lobotomy

Surgery and Showmanship

In modern psychology labs and clinics, the name Walter Free-man is synonymous with recklessness and the overuse of under-tested methods. In more neurologically oriented circles, there is a polarized debate around his practices, just as there was nearly 100 years ago when he first began to practice psych-iatry. On one side of the debate are those who believe that sur-gical procedures involving the brain should only be considered as an absolute last resort when no other treatment option has been effective. To *intentionally* cause brain damage would be abhorrent and unacceptable. This is the most prevalent side of the debate, with modern arguments including the many var-ieties of medications now available to treat biochemical dis-orders. In Freeman's days, this side would also include psychoanalysts, or those who followed the newly developed theories of Sigmund Freud. In opposition, the biological and more surgically oriented physicians argued that since plenty of evidence exists that errant or inappropriate connections between brain regions can lead to neurological disorders, then surgical intervention and removal or resection of those connec-tions can heal such disorders. Most modern neuroscientists can agree to some degree, but will be far more likely to confirm that yes, surgery can improve outcomes, but it should still be reserved as the last possible option in preference to medications and non-pharmacological options. The extremists, those who believe that it is essentially better to try it and fail than to not have tried at all, are a small minority and include Walter Free-man himself.

So, what exactly did Walter Freeman do to warrant such a reputation as an extremist, and was there any merit to his methods? The grandson of the famous physician William W. Keen, Freeman was a unique figure; tall and bearded with a flair for the dramatic and a love of fame and attention (El-Hai, 2005). He was never described as a team player, preferring to act first and see what happened. His hope at the start of his medical career was to come up with a widespread solution to a rapidly growing number of hospitalized mental patients. With improving medical treatments, more people were surviving in the aftermath of World War I, and many of them returned home with syphilis, an infection that eventually spread into the brain. Patients would then go into the hospital, and most often only left through the morgue. Freeman's goal to reduce these numbers and send more people home therefore indicate that he began his venture with the best intentions in mind. Surely enough, the most common issue people today have with him is the road he took to reach his goals, and the extremes to which he took his methods.

Freeman was deeply inspired by another pioneering neuroscientist, the Portuguese neurosurgeon Egas Moniz, and his partner, Almeida Lima. In 1936, the European team began publishing reports of their experimentation with human surgical resection of the fibers connecting the thalamus (the brain's main relay center) to the frontal lobe. They called it the prefrontal leucotomy, named for both the brain region targeted by the procedure, and the specialized instruments used to do so (El-Hai, 2005; Dolan, 2007; Getz, 2009; Balcells, 2014). The procedure was inspired by studies by Dr. Fulton of London, in which chimpanzees whose frontal lobe connections had been severed showed significant reductions in agitation and mood disturbances. When attempted in humans with mental disturbances, about a third of patients achieved total relief of symptoms, a third achieved partial relief, and a third showed no improvement whatsoever (El-Hai, 2005; Caruso & Sheehan, 2017). Subjectively a very low number that would not be considered satisfactory to modern medicine, it was still an incredible improvement over the 0 percent recovery often reported by inpatient mental hospitals at the time. Freeman was confident that this was the way to help people. He wrote to his role model with laudatory remarks, receiving gratitude in return, and ordered some custom leucotomes himself, partnering with the much more stoic surgeon,

James Watts, to begin performing prefrontal leucotomies in the United States, eventually renaming them lobotomies in reference to the disconnection[1] of the frontal lobe.

The prefrontal lobotomy as designed by Moniz and adapted by Freeman entailed shaving the front half of the skull, and carefully boring a series of holes on both the left and right side above the frontal lobe (El-Hai, 2005). The leucotome would be inserted to a specified depth, and a loupe extended from the handle and rotated to create controlled cuts in the area at the point of the instrument. The tool would then be removed, reinserted at different angles, and another cut made. This act of cutting a loop of tissue was called 'coring', and typically ranged from three to six cores in early tests (Balcells, 2014). Depending on the severity of his patients' symptoms, Freeman would make more or fewer cuts to the frontal lobe. One patient in 1936 diagnosed with 'agitated depression' received as many as 18 cuts to the brain (12 was standard), dying of hemorrhage when a vessel was cut during the procedure (El-Hai, 2005). While disappointed and mourning the loss of his patient, Freeman continued undeterred.

Freeman faced criticism right off the bat, including from his closest colleague, Dr. Watts. Rather than being widely accepted and practiced as is shown in popular media and cinema, only a comparative small number of physicians adopted his techniques. Most often, the lobotomy was criticized as an unnecessary and dangerous (major blood vessels occasionally ruptured and endangered patients, as in the 1936 case), and while Freeman himself often performed major aspects of the surgeries himself, he was not a surgeon; he was a psychiatrist (El-Hai, 2005). He also possessed a disregard for sterile technique (a later colleague was quoted as arguing to at least let them drape the patient before they began), and was hesitant to report on the less-desirable effects on patients who would not be considered success stories. He even developed what he called the 'jiffy spinal tap', which cut down the time and effort of traditional spinal taps by utilizing the cisterna magna, a cavity of cerebrospinal fluid at the base of the skull (El-Hai, 2005; Dolan, 2007; Dully & Fleming, 2007). This speedy version, rather than slowly inserting a needle between spinal vertebrae, had a patient bend their head over the back of a chair while the needle was inserted between the spine and skull, dangerously close to the life-supporting brainstem. By either sheer luck or steadiness of hand,

Freeman never reported any mistakes or slips of the needle into the brainstem, yet no other physician on record has since been willing to risk attempting it.

Criticisms aside, the scientific community had to admit that there were a number of people who reported great improvements after having had lobotomies. Freeman's first patient, Alice Hammat, was wracked with anxiety and agitation related to obsessive-compulsive traits, and awoke from her surgery with no apparent worries to report; she 'felt great!' (El-Hai, 2005). She required a bit more assistance from her husband and her maid, but was overall far better off than she had been, a result that lasted for years. At the advice of Moniz, Freeman kept track of his patients for years afterward, and would later donate his records to George Washington University archives. Many others in these records reported similar satisfactions, including a young daughter whose mother was so much improved by lobotomy that the girl was no longer afraid of her. Contact and compassion toward his patients would accumulate over time to the point where he frequently received Christmas cards from grateful recipients. By the end of World War II, however, the prefrontal lobotomy was no longer enough to keep up with the rising number of mental patients in the US.

Again inspired by the experiments of a European scientist, Amarro Fiamberti of Italy, entering the skull through the thin bone at the back of the orbit, or eye socket, was less dangerous than boring multiple holes in the top of the skull, and avoided major structures like the frontal sinus (El-Hai, 2005). Fiamberti would inject alcohol or formalin to destroy tissue without the risk of cutting blood vessels, though he occasionally would insert a leucotome for more severe cases. Eventually, Fiamberti lost interest in the procedure, but Freeman had latched onto it as strongly as he had Moniz's original technique. With the theory that distal atrophy of the thalamus and its connections would have the same basic effect as traditional lobotomies, Freeman refined the technique, seeking stronger instruments that would pierce the skull without fracturing bone, leaving minimal damage. He eventually tested an ice pick from his kitchen drawer and found it to be perfectly suited for the job. Unlike other surgical instruments with odd nicknames, this is unfortunately not a metaphor; it was a literal ice pick with the brand name 'Uline Ice Company' embossed on the handle. If it's strange, but it works, it isn't strange anymore …

The procedure for the newly coined transorbital lobotomy is not for the faint of heart.[2] The so-called 'anesthetic' was a few pulses of electroshock, essentially to induce a stupor, followed by careful placement of the pick, which he redesigned into an orbitoclast, between the eye and the orbit wall. The tool would then be not-so-delicately hammered through the skull to a depth of 7 centimeters from the upper eyelid, tilted 15–20 degrees toward the center and 30 degrees to the side, and slowly removed while pressure was applied to the eye to prevent bleeding (El-Hai, 2005). It would then be repeated on the other side, the whole treatment being completed in under 15 minutes for a fraction of the cost of traditional lobotomies. Eventually, he would tap into his showmanship and began doing the procedure on both sides simultaneously, often stopping mid-procedure for photographs, and in one occasion using a mallet for dramatic effect rather than his usual small metal hammer (Dully & Fleming, 2007). Patients were left with black eyes and temporary 'reverse boy scout virtues', failure to participate in such behaviors as friendliness, courtesy, and cleanliness, which would resolve after a couple of weeks. The technique would be marketed to countless mental hospitals as an affordable way to relieve patients' symptoms when they were not severe enough to merit full lobotomies, but were severe enough to interfere with the patients' lives. It was also marketed as a treatment for severe, chronic pain. To the chagrin of his already ruffled critics, Freeman often performed the transorbital lobotomies himself in a regular office, resulting in a fallout between him and his colleague Watts, who would not be a part of it unless it were done in a sterile surgical suite under the hands of a trained surgeon.

Though the creation of new medications in the 1950s, such as the antipsychotic chlorpromazine (trade name Thorazine) and other sedatives, saw a major decline in the use of brain surgery as a treatment option, Freeman continued to promote his transorbital lobotomy. Already known to be dramatic and defensive, he is reported to have thrown a box of hundreds of cards of patient correspondence onto a table during a presentation in 1960 when he was criticized for performing the procedure on children (Dully & Fleming, 2007). Freeman's use of lobotomies to treat mental illness is recorded to have finally ended as late as in 1967 with the death of a repeat customer and the revocation of his surgical privileges from Herrick Memorial Hospital (El-

Hai, 2005). He continued to travel and correspond with his former patients until his own death in 1972 after a recurrent battle with colon cancer.

Yet the story is not quite over. After the release of his patient records and a special report from a lobotomy survivor in 2004 (broadcast on NPR), the details from decades of American lobotomies began to spread and are still being uncovered as more patients, victims, and family members speak out about the effects of a surgery intended to cause brain damage. As originally suspected, the lack of visualization during surgery limited the precision of the procedure, and led to significant differences in post-surgical symptoms from one patient to another.

Frontal Lobe Syndrome

After having had a frontal lobotomy of either type, patients were often said to be affected by frontal lobe syndrome (FLS). In some cases, Freeman claimed that this would pass, though they may experience episodes of remission into their previous problematic behaviors (El-Hai, 2005). Often, it did not pass, though, and despite reporting relief of emotional distress, the FLS symptoms remained. With significant overlaps and comorbidities with dementia, FLS includes behavioral and emotional, or affective, symptoms (Gislason et al., 2003). Affective symptoms include emotional blunting, which may be described as a major goal of Freeman's lobotomies, as well as apathy and neglect of behaviors such as hygiene. Behavioral symptoms include but are not limited to loss of tact or sense of appropriateness, inflexibility or stubbornness, hypersexuality, inappropriate humor,[3] and impaired judgment. Among the most famous individuals with FLS is Phineas Gage, whose most pronounced symptoms were, of course, changes to his personality and impaired behavioral regulation (Gislason et al., 2003; Dolan, 2007). Also similar to Gage, a number of Freeman's patients would develop convulsions and seizures, though it is unclear whether these were due to the lobotomy itself or, in early stages, due to the application of electroshock.

Famous Patients

Freeman himself performed thousands of lobotomies in one form or another, an estimated 3000 lobotomies in 23 states, and trained

many others in how to do the procedures (El-Hai, 2005; Dully &
Fleming, 2007; Balcells, 2014). So, it is of no surprise that some
significant names would fall under the points of his leucotomes.
Rose Williams, the schizophrenic sister of playwright Tennessee
Williams, received a prefrontal lobotomy in the early 1940s by
a Missouri doctor, Paul Schrader (El-Hai, 2005). Frances Farmer,
an American actress, was rumored to have received a lobotomy by
Freeman himself, which is depicted in the film *Frances*, though no
documented evidence exists to support the suggestion that she had
a lobotomy at all. Whether famous by their own respects or made
famous by their experiences, the following individuals are among
the most well known of Freeman's own collection of patients.

Rosemary Kennedy. Eldest sister of deceased president John
F. Kennedy Jr., Rosemary was generally hidden away from the
public eye to spare the famous family some unwanted embarrassment. Considered initially to be the prettiest Kennedy
sister, Rosemary was mentally slow due to a complication at
birth. While being delivered, a doctor was not readily available,
so the infant was forced to remain in the birth canal for two
hours, depriving her brain of critical oxygen and slowing her
mental development (WHL, 2019). Still able to function rather
well, learning to read and write and participate in social
events, Rosemary eventually developed some reckless behaviors
as a young adult. By the age of 23, she displayed trouble controlling her anger, outbursts of emotion, and disinhibition,
sneaking out at night and returning later with her clothes
a mess (El-Hai, 2005). Despite her intellectual disability, Freeman considered her an excellent candidate for lobotomy, and
in 1941, with the support of her father but without any notifi-
cation to her mother Rose, Rosemary Kennedy received an
aggressive prefrontal lobotomy. She received a mild tranquil-
izer, and her brain was operated on while she remained conscious, even being asked to sing 'God Bless America' so that
Freeman knew when to stop (when she was unable to continue,
it was deep enough, and he would stop the cut) (El-Hai, 2005;
Dolan, 2007; WHL, 2019).

Rosemary Kennedy's operation would prove too aggressive.
Rather than reducing her emotional outbursts and controlling
her reckless behaviors, the procedure left her with the mental
capacity of a toddler, and she was unable to live with even partial independence (El-Hai, 2005; WHL, 2019). She was admitted

to an institution and remained there for the rest of her life, generally forgotten and hidden away from the public. Her own family remained overall separated from her, and the lobotomy was not publicly admitted; it was instead claimed that she was admitted for her intellectual disabilities. As a silver lining to her tragic tale, however, Rosemary's story would inspire her sister Eunice Kennedy Shriver to start the Special Olympics programs, and encourage thousands of other impaired individuals to display their strengths proudly.

Ellen Ionesco. Made famous by virtue of being Freeman's first transorbital patient, Ellen Ionesco was suffering from symptoms that would today be compared to bipolar disorder, or manic depression. The young mother would have depressive episodes that kept her in bed for weeks, intermingled with bouts of mania that featured spasms of violence, which harmed her then four year old daughter, and recurring thoughts and attempts at suicide (El-Hai, 2005). The procedure was deemed a success, in that her outbursts were gone, and there was peace at home. Her daughter, Angelene Forester, would later report on the relief she felt as a child, but concern as an adult, as her mother was not quite there anymore for a long time after the operation. She was able to make a fairly good recovery, though, becoming a nurse, working steadily, and participating in social events with their church and neighbors.

Howard Dully. In stark contrast to the reported successes of Mrs. Ionesco, Howard Dully's experience with the famed lobotomist was not one of comfort and relief. Unable to truly resolve what he had been through for 40 years after, Dully eventually sought answers, producing a radio broadcast with NPR in 2004 and publishing a book about his experiences called *My Lobotomy* (Dully & Fleming, 2007). Like Rosemary Kennedy, Dully became a candidate based on the testimony of a family member. Unlike Rosemary, however, Dully was not exactly showing the behaviors that had been reported to Freeman during his assessment. For yet unknown reasons, Dully's stepmother, Lou, was determined to remove the boy from her family, subjecting him to years of emotional and physical abuse. She sought help from several psychiatrists, all of whom told her that the problem was not the boy, it was *her.* Unhappy with those answers, she went to Freeman, feeding him information that was greatly exaggerated by her own obsessive thoughts, and even lying behind his father's back by telling Freeman that the boy had viciously attacked his mentally impaired infant brother. He had not, of course. He was just a young man who wanted to be loved by his family. He met with Freeman, whom he described as being warm and attentive, and eventually was approved for a transorbital lobotomy. Lou took two months convincing Freeman to do the operation, and two days convincing her husband. Howard Dully was 12 years old.

In the aftermath of the lobotomy, Dully has gaps in his memory. His brother described him as looking somewhat like a zombie, sitting upright in bed with no expression on his face. Reports state he was more agreeable and less aggressive than before, but Lou was still unhappy with his presence in the home. He was sent from place to place, including foster care, juvenile detention, an asylum, and a special school for impaired teens. He was homeless on multiple occasions, dappled in illicit drugs and alcohol, and generally struggled to survive. He was not given the opportunity to finish his high school degree, later opting to educate himself when he was able to get his life on track. Always trying to hide the shame he felt at having received a lobotomy, he was eventually encouraged to talk about it, meeting with other former patients of Freeman and breaking down the stigma of life after lobotomy. He cannot change what had been done to him by an unloving stepmother, but through communication, he and other survivors can ensure that such things do not happen again to other innocent kids.

Helen Mortensen. The idea of a single lobotomy is abhorrent to most people today, but to Helen Mortensen, it was a godsend. She was among the first ten people to receive a transorbital lobotomy from Freeman in 1946, and experienced a near total relief of her depressive symptoms. Ten years later, her symptoms relapsed, so she returned to him for a refresher, and again felt a relief of symptoms. Another eight years passed, and Mortensen relapsed once more, returning to Freeman yet again for her miracle cure. Unfortunately, this was to be both her and his last lobotomy. A blood vessel ruptured during the procedure, and Mortensen died three days later as a direct result of the hemorrhage (El-Hai, 2005). One other patient who received a lobotomy the same day fared well, but Freeman was finished. Herrick Memorial Hospital, where he had moved his practice after leaving George Washington University in DC, revoked his operating room privileges, and Freeman officially retired, choosing instead to travel and follow up on other patients for the remainder of his life.

Modern Methods

After the fall of the lobotomy, treatments for mental illness shifted predictably toward medications and psychotherapy instead of surgery. Operating on the brain was again to be reserved to last-resort cases that did not respond to therapy or medications. Those who believed in surgical intervention remained, though, and more strict experimentation on therapeutic brain surgeries began. Through carefully regulated and tested trials, a number of new techniques have been developed for use today. Still withheld until all other avenues have failed, modern brain surgery, aside from the removal of tumors and diseased tissues, is now effective for treatment-resistant depression, epilepsy, obsessive-compulsive disorders, and even Parkinson's disease.

The closest to lobotomy in technique is the corpus callosotomy, also known as the split-brain procedure, or cutting of the dense white matter tract that connects the two hemispheres of the brain (Kolb & Wishaw, 2009; Pinel & Barnes, 2018). Callosotomy is used for severe epilepsy that does not respond to anticonvulsants, particularly temporal lobe epilepsy, in which the seizures become life-threatening. Other surgeries are less for cutting connections and more for stimulating and increasing functional activity in the brain, as in deep brain stimulation (DBS). In DBS, thin metal electrodes are implanted into specific brain areas to provide electrical stimulation depending on what symptoms the patient is presenting. For Parkinsonism, the subthalamic nucleus or globus pallidus is stimulated to reduce resting tremors and increase voluntary control of movement. For severe depression and OCD, areas being tested for efficacy include the ventral capsule/ventral striatum and nucleus accumbens (Borders et al., 2018). Based on this last finding, perhaps Freeman was not so far off in his theories regarding lobotomies' efficacy, though it can still be argued that his methods were a bit too aggressive.

Additional Remarks

Despite his many criticisms, Freeman is not to be villainized. He meant the best when he followed through with his procedures. If a family member objected to the procedure, he would not do it. All patients who reported interactions with him described him as a warm and kind man who put them at ease and was comfortable to be around. While his aggressive approach to brain surgery gives him a less than pleasant reputation, Freeman's high number of lobotomy patients and detailed documentation provided a font of information regarding the function of the frontal lobe, and may have even contributed to modern approaches to treating drug-resistant emotional disorders. Surely there must be a fine balance between talk therapies, medications, and biological interventions. Perhaps when we finally find that balance, there will no longer be a need for the dramatic experimental attempts used in years gone by.

Notes

1 A key difference between the stereotypical lobotomy and other procedures called lobectomies, the -otomy suffix refers to transection or cutting of tissues, whereas an -ectomy suffix refers to removal of tissue. Therefore, a lobectomy removes a section of tissue, such as when removing tumors or infections, while the lobotomy leaves all tissue in place, but cuts the white matter tracts within it.

2 The procedure was, in fact, so disturbing to watch that many observers have described it as 'horrifying'. One particular moment of great pride for Freeman was during a demonstration in which an observing emeritus professor was so shocked that he fainted.

3 The use or enjoyment of inappropriate humor is related to and may even overlap with a disorder called Witzelsucht, a compulsion to tell awful puns and jokes constantly or at bad times, such as during a funeral. While entertaining to read about, Witzelsucht is very distressful to those around the affected person.

Chapter 8

'Hi, My Name is Henry'

The World's Most Memorable Amnestic, H.M.

Living Only in the Here and Now

Any text on the history of neuroscience would be remiss to forget to discuss H.M., and nearly every modern textbook in psychology contains at least a sidebar on him, if not more. In 1953, a 27-year-old man with a prolonged history of severe seizures received a radical new surgery to reduce his risk of a life-threatening incident. He subsequently entered the history books not due to the success of the surgery, but due to its side effects. From the day of his surgery onward, Henry Molaison, often referred to as H.M. to protect his privacy during life, could no longer form any conscious long-term memories whatsoever.

The procedure, described by surgeon W. B. Scoville as a 'frankly experimental operation', was not undertaken lightly, but was done as a last resort when no other available treatment option had been effective in reducing Henry's seizures. Having sustained a minor head injury at about age nine with no major symptoms other than having blacked out,[1] the boy began to have seizures regularly, beginning with petit mal by age ten, and advancing to full-blown grand mal seizures before age 16 (Scoville & Milner, 1957; Corkin, 2013). Comparatively less dramatic than the stereotypical grand mal, or tonic-clonic seizures (named for the rigid muscle tone and tremors associated with them), petit mal seizures are often called 'absence seizures' because the person affected appears to go mentally absent from an observer's perspective. To the untrained eye, an absence seizure may appear that a person's attention has drifted off into a daydream, or that they have fallen asleep in their seat for a moment. Occasionally, a seizure may also include automatisms or repetitive movements, such as buttoning and unbuttoning a shirt or scratching at one's skin. When the seizure finally abates, the person may appear dazed or sleepy, like shaking off fatigue. Some may be temporarily unable to speak or walk for a short time afterward (Anonymous, 2017). In Henry's case, he would seem to tune out, breathe heavily, and scratch lightly at his arms, then shake it off with a calm remark. The onset of grand mal seizures with frightening convulsions and the loss of consciousness was a sure sign that his condition was worsening over time. They also meant that his already shy nature in school was made worse by the embarrassment that the poorly understood disorder held. Still, Henry was seen as calm and polite, though he mostly kept to himself and to a couple of close friends (Corkin, 2013).

As Henry's seizures progressed, the medications he took to control them also increased to overwhelming levels. By age 26, he was taking regular doses of four different anti-seizure medications, including Dilantin, Phenobarbital, Tridione, and Mesantoin (Corkin, 2013). It was clear that something else needed to be done before a prolonged seizure injured him, or worse, took his life. At this time, he met with the neurosurgeon Dr. Scoville, who had been researching a procedure developed by Wilder Penfield which resected, or removed, portions of the medial temporal lobe to reduce the frequency and intensity of intractable seizures, those which do not respond to typical treatments or medications. The team ran several tests in an attempt to identify the point of origin for the seizures, but were unsuccessful. Ironically, this made Henry an excellent candidate for the procedure. Unable to determine whether the seizures were beginning in the left or right hemisphere, Henry was scheduled for a bilateral resection of the amygdala, hippocampal gyrus, and the uncus of the temporal lobe (Figure 8.1).

In light of the now receding support for psychosurgery after the fall of the prefrontal lobotomy, Scoville carefully considered alternatives and methods for minimizing the damage caused by the surgery. To avoid disturbing blood vessels and brain areas associated with personality, he would bore two windows in the front of the skull (a craniotomy) and carefully raise the frontal lobe to provide a better line of sight to the temporal lobes, removing the offending tissue with a combination of scalpel cuts and suction, planned to go as far as 8 cm from the front curvature of the temporal lobe

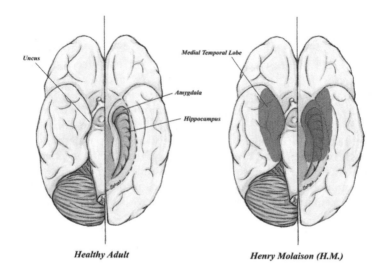

Healthy Adult   *Henry Molaison (H.M.)*

Figure 8.1 A cross-section of the ventral surface of a healthy, neurotypical brain compared to the regions scheduled to be excised in Henry Molaison's 'frankly experimental surgery'. Regions targeted in the procedure included the amygdala, hippocampal gyrus, and the uncus of the temporal lobe. The surgery would significantly reduce his seizure activity, but leave him with extremely limited memory capabilities, especially for the formation of new, conscious memories.

(Scoville & Milner, 1957). Henry's surgery was considered a success, carried out under only local anesthetic so that speech and motor areas were not damaged,[2] and they encountered no complications. After the surgery, however, was another story.

Henry did continue to have seizures after his surgery, though they were far less severe and were less frequent. In this regard, the surgery was a success. He even appeared to have a higher IQ than before, though this may have been due to improved concentration and a reduction in sedating anti-seizure medications (Scoville & Milner, 1957; Corkin, 2013). He also showed no major changes to his personality, and remained his usual kind and patient self. The biggest issue appeared when he was expected to remember basically anything beyond 30 seconds ago. For 55 years, Henry would continue to report no known knowledge of anything after the time of his surgery. Other patients in his cohort (a group of peers receiving similar treatments around the same time) also experienced amnesia, but it appeared to affect only those who had bilateral resections or whose hippocampus opposite the one resected was damaged. For instance, two fellow epileptics referred to as F.C. and P.B. received only unilateral resections of the left hippocampi, but were found to have sustained damage to their right hippocampi as a result of their chronic seizures. This made their cases a bit more complicated compared to Henry's, whose results were so pure and clearly defined between pre- and post-surgery that he was certain to prove invaluable to the scientific community.

Fortunately for the eager research teams involved in Henry's case, he remained as polite and cooperative as ever, happily participating in whatever tasks were asked of him. He rapidly became a favorite of researchers and caregivers alike, often getting spoiled with extra food and treats, though he was unable to tell you what he had eaten, or if he had already eaten, other than the fact that he did not like liver. When asked to make sure he remembered something, Henry would be able to do so, within limits. For example, when asked to track how long a researcher had been out of the room, he mentally recited to himself the time until they returned, at which time he did some quick mental math to answer the question (Corkin, 2013). If, however, his attention were disrupted at any time during this mental rehearsal, he would lose the information entirely and forget that any question were asked of him at all. Common memory tests Henry showed impairments in typically utilize a delay or some sort of interference to test a person's short-term or working memory, estimated in large part thanks to Henry as being about 20–30 seconds long. Others may also show impairments in these tests if there is a deficit in attentional processing, as seen in dementias like Alzheimer's disease, since the brain is unable to hang onto and rehearse information as efficiently as it once did. Yet with as much as Henry was unable to remember, it is what he *could* do that gained him even more attention, and pioneered new discoveries in memory and learning.

With such a profoundly affected memory system, Henry was unable to live on his own, depending first on his parents and then on family friends for assistance. To some degree, he was able to work with a neighborhood program that supplied work for the mentally disabled, though his supervisors noted that if a task had more than three steps, he could not remember how to complete the work. His mother, however, insisted over time that his memory seemed to be improving slightly. Researchers initially turned down this idea as a mother's optimism until later on when caregivers noted that he knew things that he 'had no business knowing' given his condition. When it was formally tested, it was finally apparent that Henry indeed could remember things; he just had no idea that he was remembering them. Today this would be delineated into declarative versus nondeclarative memory systems. Henry lived with a complete loss of his declarative memory, meaning that he could not declare or state that he remembered something. His nondeclarative memory, however, had bits and pieces that it could hang onto, particularly motor tasks and occasionally visual familiarity. For example, when shown images and names of celebrities who became popular only after his surgery, then asked to match those faces with the correct names, Henry could somewhat accurately pair them, and would often say to repeat visitors that he knew them, but could not remember where from. Researcher and frequent visitor Suzanne Corkin, for example, states that Henry often insisted that they must have known each other from high school, since she was so closely familiar to him '(Corkin, 2013).

Motor skills that Henry learned are particularly interesting, in that he showed improvements in time and accuracy for tests such as the mirror-drawing task, rotary pursuit, and a target-practice style game that he took to like a kid in an arcade. For most of the tests, he seemed surprised at how well he had done, stating that he expected it to be more difficult than it was, and insisting that he could not remember ever having tried it before. It must be incredible beginner's luck. These, as well as tests in classical conditioning such as the eyeblink test, in which air is puffed into the eye following a tone until the tone itself elicits a blink of the eyes, showed such near-normal scores that it was quite apparent that brain areas other than the medial temporal lobe were responsible for motor and habit learning, including the cortex, basal ganglia, and cerebellum. Henry's cerebellum was somewhat atrophied and smaller than average, likely damaged by the heavy use of anticonvulsant medications to control his seizures, and his reaction times reflected this, yet when given enough time to complete his task, he was quite capable of utilizing it and the rest of his cortex for what we now call procedural memory. Similar to the term 'motor memory', procedural memory is a subtype of nondeclarative memory dedicated to sequences of movements, such as riding a bike, navigating your neighborhood on the way home, or even brushing your teeth. When learning these things, we must pay active attention to each step, but once a task is well-learned, it is shifted to a more automatic form of processing, reflected also in a shift in brain areas, and we begin to perform them without full awareness. We sit on the bike and pedal, our car seems to take us home on its own, and we put toothpaste on the brush. Henry, like most others, could perform these tasks just fine (other than driving a car, as his seizures precluded this). But for many affected by dementias, steps may be missed. We may forget which direction to push the bike pedals in, a yellow traffic light goes unseen, and the wrong side of the toothbrush gets paste on it. Once noticed, such seemingly silly errors may be either brushed off or incite great distress. But like Henry's difficulty in declarative memory, it is simply beyond our brain's remaining controls.

Memory was eventually found to not be the only area that Henry possessed deficits in. Over time, scientists and caregivers noticed that Henry never really expressed that he was hungry, thirsty, or in pain, and began to wonder if he felt them to a lesser degree than others. When he went without lunch, he would not comment until somebody insisted that he must be hungry. If brought a second lunch, he would gladly eat it without expressing that he was too full for more. He would get irritable at times, but would not express sensations of pain, nor did he show any indications of romantic desires. To answer this, they looked toward another area targeted in his surgery: the amygdala and nearby hypothalamus. Now known to play major roles in emotion as well as memory, the amygdala is closely connected also to pain processing (including emotional pain), and Henry's were almost completely removed. To compensate for this, caregivers attempted to be more scheduled and attentive for his diet, water intake, and physical health. Yet, after decades of priceless contributions to science, Henry's active testing days had to come to an inevitable end.

In December of 2008, after a relatively rapid decline, Henry Molaison succumbed to respiratory failure at the age of 82, some 55 years after losing his sense of the future. After protecting his privacy for these decades by referring to him only as H.M., the research teams finally released his name to the world. But his contributions were not quite over yet. His research teams were called upon once more, this time to collect and examine his most priceless possession: his brain. Working through the night, the team scanned, imaged, and preserved the precious brain, preparing it for the long process of chemical histology (Carey, 2008; Corkin, 2013). One year after his death, the 53-hour long process of sectioning (cutting) Henry's brain into 70-micron thin slices took place, with the research team filming and live-streaming the procedure over the internet to 400,000 viewers. The ultimate results, ever adding to the field Henry had already helped to build, are now readily available for free to those interested through the Brain Observatory (2018).

Finally, nearly 60 years after his fateful surgery, we had full visual and microscopic evidence of the damage done to Henry's brain. Scoville had targeted as much as 8 cm of tissue beginning at the front-most curvature of the temporal lobe, intended to excise the uncus, amygdala, and hippocampal complex. What was found upon autopsy was instead *less* extensive than planned, affecting primarily the polar cortex of the medial temporal lobe, most of the amygdalae and entorhinal cortex, and about half of the hippocampus nearest to the ventricles, including the dentate gyrus and subiculum sub-areas (Annese et al., 2014). Surrounding areas seemed largely unaffected, and the surgical site was symmetrical, as Scoville had planned. To some, the sizeable remaining hippocampus may be surprising, though it is suggested that the entorhinal cortex, the cortical area below and adjacent to the hippocampus that was almost completely removed, serves as a connection between the hippocampus and other cortical areas, explaining the apparent disconnect between Henry's memory system and the rest of his brain.

Generations of researchers continue to learn from Henry's brain. The work stemming from his contributions has bolstered our knowledge of multiple systems of memory, from his intact short-term memory and cognition, including perception, to his lack of consolidation of new memories from short to long-term, and his continued growth in non-declarative memories. Even unexpected findings such as the brain areas associated with odor recognition, the parahippocampal gyrus, amygdala, and adjacent cortex, were identified thanks in part to Henry (Annese et al., 2014). Henry left behind no living relatives, but an immeasurable legacy in the science of learning and memory.

Alternative Treatments

While treatment options for severe, treatment-resistant epilepsy are still comparatively small in number, the identification of less obvious seizures such as absence seizures has greatly improved in the decades since Henry's surgery, as have techniques for identifying the points of origins for generalized seizures. As in the majority of other conditions, there is likely not going to be any single cure-all for epilepsy. Instead, treatments should be considered on a case-by-case basis based on the age of the individual, their types and frequencies of seizure, and responsiveness to medication. New and less-sedating medications are now available to help manage seizure severity, and trained support animals can readily identify a coming seizure so that their human can get to safety or take emergency medication before onset. If these options still fail, a few specialized surgical options remain available.

Focal Resection. Henry's medial temporal lobectomy is considered to be a form of resection, albeit a very broad rather than focal one. Still, the resection of brain tissue was effective for a number of people even in Henry's cohort if held to smaller and more specific areas. In order to determine the point of origin for Henry's seizures, his doctors utilized electroencephalogram (EEG) recordings as well as pneumoencephalograms, contrast x-rays of the brain that visualize oxygen as it travels through the cerebrospinal fluid canals. One potential issue with this is that whole-brain EEGs tend to measure an overall level of activity over a shallow portion of the entire cortex, rather than showing specific regions of activity spikes. More modern methods have added in the use of intracranial EEGs, or measurements of activity from within the brain rather than over the scalp. While significantly more invasive than scalp electrodes, intracranial EEG is able to detect regional spikes such as high-frequency oscillations and fast ripples, providing a more thorough estimate of the seizure onset zone (Akiyama et al., 2011). Paired with direct cortical stimulation, or the stimulation of specific brain zones to detect their function (used often to locate language areas so as not to damage them during surgery), the target area can be planned ahead of time, and the offending area resected with minimal damage. Initial testing showed promising trends in relieving patients' worst seizures; follow-up studies have observed few major complications as a result of the intracranial EEGS, the most common being CSF leak, which resolves itself over time, and following the resection itself, minor visual field interruptions that may not be readily noticed unless pointed out through neurological testing (Hader et al., 2013). Such side effects and others are, of course, necessary to discuss, but do not tend to be severe enough to discard focal resection as a therapeutic option. If there is a possibility for seizure-free life, many would take the smaller risk rather than continue on less effective management techniques. Yet for those who still find the removal of brain tissue aversive, there are other viable surgical options available.

The 'Split-Brain' Procedure. Initially characterized by van Wagenen in 1940, the so-called 'split-brain' surgery to treat intractable epilepsy lost favor until its resurgence decades later with Sperry and Gazzaniga's successful follow-up procedures (van Wagenen & Herren, 1940; Mathews et al., 2008). The procedure was based on the principal concept that the corpus callosum, the massive body of white matter that transmits information between the left and right hemispheres, also transmits seizure activities between the temporal lobes. Theoretically, severing this connection would also cut off the potential for a small focal seizure to spread and become a global seizure. Seven of ten initial patients showed significant improvements after having the callosum partially or fully cut, with larger cuts showing more dramatic reductions in seizure activity. Why a gap in time followed the discovery of the procedure is not clear, though in the years following Henry's temporal lobectomy, the split-brain procedure, formally called a corpus callosotomy, began its refinement. Still only recommended as a last resort when other treatments have been found ineffective, callosotomy now has a low mortality and high success rate, particularly for young people and those who experience atonic/tonic seizures, or those featuring a loss of muscle tone, or 'drop attack', or increase in muscle tone, such as stiffness (Asadi-Pooya et al., 2008; Tanriverdi et al., 2009). In particularly severe cases, a complete callosotomy can be done, which severs the entire white matter body, though this can result in a condition known as disconnection syndrome, in which the two hemispheres are no longer able to communicate, and the non-verbal or non-dominant hand seems to operate on its own without the owner's conscious awareness (occasionally nicknamed 'Alien Hand Syndrome'). Partial resection, on the other hand, can still have highly effective results while reducing the risk of such disruptive adverse effects. The recommended resection for most viable candidates is the anterior two-thirds, closest to the front of the head, leaving the posterior splenium portion of the structure intact to assist with healthy hemispheric communication. Like Henry's case, intelligence seems largely unaffected by the surgery. Unlike Henry's case, patients with memory difficulties post-operation are the minority. However, the callosotomy is still not a miracle cure, as many will continue to experience seizures at reduced frequency and severity, and those with myoclonic seizures (featuring muscle jerks) tend not to improve much. Whether Henry would have benefited from the split-brain procedure or not can only be speculated, though it is likely that he would have done well. Yet we would certainly have lost one of the most treasured brains of modern neuroscience. Clearly, Henry's loss was our gain.

Future Research

Despite his own memory deficits, Henry Molaison is, to the worlds of neuroscience and psychology, completely unforgettable. Those who knew him and worked with him adored him, and those who simply read about him were stunned by his story. We have learned innumerable facts about the human memory system from him, though we have plenty left to learn. Using him as a model for 'hippocampus-dependent learning', we have seen that animals with damaged hippocampi are still somehow capable of learning such dependent tasks. Where in the cortex are such memories stored? How are older memories more resistant to forgetting than newer ones? Is there a physical change similar to LTP that occurs between recent long-term memories and distant long-term memories? If we are to learn half as much in the next 50 years as we did during Henry's last 50 years, then surely we may be able to answer some, if not all, of these questions.

Notes

1   The exact source of his epilepsy was unknown, but suspected to be the result of a run-in with a bicycle. It is unclear whether he had been struck by a cyclist or had fallen off of his own bike, but either way, he had struck his head and was unconscious for a short time, about 5 minutes. Since his brain scans appeared completely normal, under

modern interpretations we can say that he sustained some level of concussion from the incident.

2 Performing brain surgeries while awake is now a standard procedure, sometimes referred to as 'awake craniotomy', since the scalp can be numbed and the brain does not itself have pain receptors. Maintaining wakefulness not only allows the patient to respond to verbal requests and test paradigms, but also removes the risk of surgical anesthetics and their hefty side effects.

Chapter 9

'To Jodie with Love'
James Brady's Emotional Journey

Saturday Night Special

In 1976, a young Jodie Foster appeared on the silver screen as a teenage prostitute in *Taxi Driver*. She was 13 years old at the time. Then 21 years old, John Hinckley Jr. was smitten. Having already experienced some issues with mental health and an enthusiastic interest in weapons, Hinckley soon became obsessed with the young actress, going so far as to follow her as she attended Yale, sending her notes and poems and calling her repeatedly over the phone. Hinckley would later be identified as having schizophrenia, with emphasis on disorganized thoughts and delusions (2019a). Others may yet suggest that he had erotomania, a delusional disorder characterized by extreme infatuation, often with one of a higher status than oneself (APA, 2013). Actors and celebrities are frequent targets of erotomaniacs' affections, though few cases are as publicized as the one between Foster and Hinckley.

After repeatedly failing to get the attention and affections of Foster, Hinckley sought drastic measures. Inspired again by *Taxi Driver*, he conspired to create a grand gesture by assassinating the president of the United States, citing that by earning himself a place in history, she would surely change her feelings toward him. Spoiler alert: It did not work. After having stalked President Carter and purchasing multiple firearms, he was arrested at Nashville for carrying concealed weapons, but was released and soon forgotten about (Taubman, 1981). Failing at executing this attempt, Hinckley retreated and would plan a new attempt at a new target: then incumbent president Ronald Reagan.

Just months into Reagan's term, on March 30, 1981, he and his team were leaving the Washington Hilton Hotel after a speech and headed toward the presidential limousine. A voice was heard calling out 'Mr. President', sparking him to turn and wave to the crowd. Shots rang out. Four men were hit: (1) Thomas Delehanty, a policeman, received partial spinal trauma and subsequent nerve damage; (2) Tim McCarthy, a service agent, was hit in the abdomen and sustained damage to several organs; (3) the president himself, Ronald Reagan, was struck in the lung when a bullet ricocheted off the armored limousine; and (4) press secretary James Brady was shot in the head (Cytowic, 1981; Reagan, 1991; Aaron & Rockoff, 1994; Hermann & Ruane, 2014). All four men survived, and Hinckley was immediately tackled and arrested. He would later be found Not Guilty by Reason of Insanity (much to the chagrin of many US citizens) and remains under supervision by mental health professionals (Hans & Slater, 1983; Hermann & Ruane, 2014; Dateline, 2019).

Brady's road to survival, however, was arguably more difficult than any of the four men. The medical team worked quickly, though certainly there was not much room for optimism. Hinckley had used a gun nicknamed the 'Saturday Night Special' loaded with Devastator bullets, specially designed to fragment on impact and spread toxic lead azide to maximize the damage done, and the one that hit Brady had shattered inside of his skull into an estimated 24 pieces (Aaron & Rockoff, 1994; Hermann & Ruane, 2014). It entered his forehead above the left eye, striking the interior right side of the skull and spreading blood and shrapnel through the right hemisphere (Figure 9.1).

Swelling and increased intracranial pressure began immediately, so surgeons administered sugars[1] and steroids to reduce the pressure and buy some time (Cytowic, 1981). A clot was rapidly forming in the temporal lobe, necessitating an emergency surgery. By the time this was decided, media reporters had snuck into the hospital to dig for information, somehow cascading to an erroneous report on national television that 'Jim Brady has died'. He had not, of course, but the emergency room is hardly a place for slow, calculated communication.

The decision the medical team made next is reminiscent of trephination: to perform a craniotomy. Pressure was building higher and higher in Brady's skull with no immediate outlet, as the site of the pressure was on the opposite side of the head as the bullet's entry wound. So, it stood to reason that the best solution was to create an outlet. A section of bone over Brady's

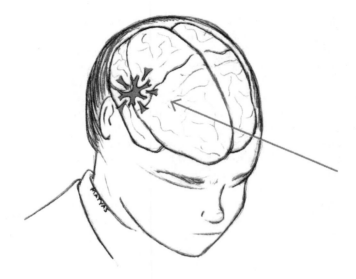

Figure 9.1 Artist's estimate for the possible trajectory of the bullet that struck Jim Brady. The .22 caliber devastator bullet, fired from a 'Saturday Night Special' revolver, entered Brady's head on the left side of his forehead above the eye, passing through the brain before it struck against the inside of the skull, fragmented, and spread shrapnel throughout the right hemisphere.

brain was removed, and the damaged tissue and blood clots were removed by suction, along with a large flattened chunk of the bullet (Cytowic, 1981). After nearly seven hours in surgery, Brady was finally deemed medically stable and could begin his long recovery. Only time could tell what Brady would have lost from the injury. With bilateral damage to his frontal lobes, and severe trauma to his right temporal and parietal lobes, the prognosis was bleak. Fortunately, James Brady possessed what others described as a 'strong, forceful personality' that kept him pushing through the therapy that was to come.

In the immediate aftermath of his injury, Brady had complete paralysis on the left side of his body, contralateral to the damage in his right motor cortex. Seizures began shortly after his first surgery and would continue throughout the remainder of his life, as would persistent pain, spasticity, and paralysis (Cytowic, 1981; Hermann & Ruane, 2014). He required numerous other surgeries for complications such as pulmonary embolism and the leakage of cerebrospinal fluid from his cranial cavity. While undergoing frequent physical and occupational therapy sessions, Brady was able to relearn walking in parallel bars and with Lofstrand crutches, yet still relied on the use of a wheelchair day-to-day. His strong personality remained fully intact, as did his sense of humor. His memory was compromised, but not severely (he would occasionally forget people's names, but easily covered it by using other cues), his sense of time and his sleep cycle were distorted, and he was easily distracted by irrelevant stimuli (Cytowic, 1981). Yet other signs commonly attributed to frontal lobe damage were either minimal or so subtle that they were virtually indistinguishable from his pre-injury self. His intelligence, as well, was determined to be as strong as it had ever been and was expected to stay that way.

Brady lived for 33 years after the shooting, advocating for firearm safety and fighting alongside his wife, Sarah, to pass The Brady Bill, legislation that would establish a minimum of a seven-day waiting period before the purchase of a handgun, thereby allowing law enforcement to run background checks and prevent the distribution of these weapons to those with criminal records or a history of mental disturbances (Reagan, 1991; Jacobs & Potter, 1995). While certainly not a perfect system, the bill would set in motion federal regulations and ignite the gun safety debates that continue today. Long after the bill was passed and signed into action, Brady continued to fight, and 30 years after the injury that cemented his name in US history, was still interviewing with reporters. After the 2011 shooting that injured Congresswoman Gabrielle Giffords in Tucson, Arizona, Brady held fast to his convictions, expressing his support for Giffords and her family, and displaying his trademark wit by quipping, 'once you've been shot in the head, it's hard to forget' (Brady, 2011; Check Hayden, 2011). In August 2014, Brady passed away from complications of his injury. The medical examiner ruled the ultimate cause of death to be homicide.

The Unexpected Effects

All things considered, Brady did remarkably well after surviving the extent of his injuries. Though his general health suffered severely and he was subject to repeated bouts of pneumonia, fevers, and seizures, his neurological health was comparatively good. There were lingering issues with memory and motor function, neither of which is unexpected, but his personality was intact, and there were no reported signs of severe depression. Another aspect of bilateral frontal lobe damage, however, is alterations in attention and emotion, as well as changes in an individual's emotional perceptions. Brady did have transient effects in alertness, and some lasting difficulty maintaining attention (Cytowic, 1981), though there is another aspect of Brady's emotional health that often goes underexamined: the emotional content of his speech. Arthur Kobrine, one of the physicians who attended Brady, described him as using a 'kind of cry-talk for a while' (Check Hayden, 2011). It is unlikely that this was a permanent effect for Brady, though for many others, it is an all too familiar and frustrating condition now known as the pseudobulbar affect (PBA).

Also known as 'pathological laughing and weeping', 'emotional lability', 'emotional incontinence', 'pathologic emotionality', 'affective instability', 'emotional dysregulation', and others depending on the specific features, pseudobulbar affect refers to the exaggeration or inconsistency of emotions that may or may not match the individual's actual emotion at the time of the episode (Schiffer & Pope, 2005; Miller et al., 2011; Ahmed & Simmons, 2013). Crying is the most common expression seen in PBA, followed by laughter. It has been identified as a comorbid disorder with amyotrophic lateral sclerosis (ALS), Parkinson's disease, multiple sclerosis, Alzheimer's, and other forms of neurotrauma, including a 5–10 percent occurrence rate in traumatic brain injuries such as Brady's. Unlike Brady's seemingly temporary experience with emotional crossover, most cases of PBA do not resolve themselves, and may even worsen as the comorbid disease progresses. In trying to identify the key brain structures involved with PBA, it has been found that lesions invariably include the bilateral motor systems, such as the internal capsules, substantia nigra, and pyramidal tracts (Schiffer & Pope, 2005), as well as the basal ganglia and cerebellum (Miller et al., 2011).

It is important to distinguish the emotional expressions of PBA from mood disorders. Mood disorders like bipolar disorder and major depression, while potentially comorbid with PBA, are more prolonged states of subjective feelings, while PBA is characterized as an affective disorder specific to the short-term, automatic emotional responses outside of individual interpretation (Miller et al., 2011). PBA has, however, responded well in the past to tricyclic antidepressants like amitriptyline, implicating the role of serotonin, while glutamate, the brain's most common excitatory neurotransmitter, is also heavily implied. The recently FDA-approved drug combination of dextromethorphan (commonly used as a cough suppressant) with quinidine (which allows the drug to remain in the system long enough to absorb at a more therapeutic dose) acts on glutamate receptors to reduce hyperactivity (Miller et al., 2011; Ahmed & Simmons, 2013). According to 'Gate-Control Theory', this hyperactivity in the brain is lowering the threshold of emotional expression, meaning that a very small amount of emotional stimulation is necessary to set off an exaggerated response. With the advent of the FDA approval of dextromethorphan/quinidine, many people have been able to feel relief or alleviation of PBA symptoms, though more work is still needed going forward.

Future Contributions

Though James and Sarah Brady are now gone, their legacy lives on, and their son Scott is sure to follow in their footsteps and continue their advocacy efforts. They, like many others affected by gun violence, long for a day where there are fewer cases like Brady's. Nonetheless, James Brady's story is one that is sure to remember and cite for years to come as we continue to study the effects of acute trauma as we did with Brady's paralysis, speech, memory, and emotions.

Note

1 The sugar in this case was the medication mannitol, which draws water from the body's cells. And since the brain is mostly water and fats, it is quite helpful for reducing intracranial swelling.

Chapter 10

'On Shaky Ground'

The Frozen Addicts and Toxin-Induced Parkinsonism

Frozen in Your Own Body

For two hundred years, we have had a well-characterized definition of Parkinson's disease (PD), or the shaking palsy. Beginning with stiffness and rigidity, progressing to tremors and difficulty walking, and ultimately leading to a near total loss of movement, there is little in the way of stopping the advance of PD, and most available therapies are palliative at best (Langston & Palfreman, 1995; Dauer & Przedborski, 2003; Pfeiffer, 2005). Symptoms do not typically appear until as much as 80 percent of the dopamine neurons in the substantia nigra brain area have been destroyed, leaving a dramatic drop in the neurotransmitter, whose role in movement as well as emotion and cognition is critical to daily function. In its more aggressive forms, PD attacks those in their 60s, but appears more often in older individuals. It was therefore all the more surprising when, in 1982, a diffuse group of young, drug-addicted individuals entered hospitals in San Jose, California, with all of the signs and symptoms of advanced, aggressive PD.

Because of the stigma surrounding drug addictions, the six various victims of the rapid-onset PD cases were all initially given incorrect diagnoses (Langston & Palfreman, 1995). One man was accused of faking his illness to get out of prison, then relabeled as a catatonic schizophrenic. His girlfriend was soon to follow him into the hospital with the same, slightly delayed, set of symptoms. A pair of brothers who had celebrated a successful drug deal by sampling their product were found by their mother frozen in place, and brought to a hospital where they, too, were marked as catatonic schizophrenics. A young mother trying to get her life on track slipped off the wagon and began using heroin again, finding herself frozen in so rigid a pose that a nerve in her leg was crushed painfully. Her case was labeled hysterical paralysis with the assurance that it was certainly all psychological in nature. Finally, a drug dealer for whom recreational drugs were a family pastime, received the closest to accurate diagnosis of the six with phenothiazine toxicity, a strong side effect from antipsychotic medications. The six would likely have been trapped in their bodies forever had one victim not been transferred to a special neurobehavioral unit for a more accurate diagnosis by a talented clinician at the Santa Clara Valley Medical Center, Bill Langston.

When Langston was called to examine a 'catatonic' patient, he knew immediately that this was not a standard case. While the individual's stiffness appeared to match waxy flexibility, a trademark of catatonic schizophrenia, the mask-like expression on his face and Myerson's sign, an alteration to the eyeblink reflex, did not match schizophrenics at all. They were more of an indication of damage to the basal ganglia, a deep-seated brain area involved in voluntary movement and habit-learning. When the man's girlfriend was then confirmed to be sick as well, Langston sought an environmental connection, perhaps in their shared apartment. The connection only got stronger when the pair of brothers was admitted to a nearby hospital with the same set of symptoms, which Langston confirmed was consistent with advanced PD. They had even responded remarkably well to levodopa (or L-Dopa), a common PD medication that increases the amount of available dopamine in the brain, alleviating symptoms. At this point, there was only one noticeable connection between the four frozen victims so far: they had all been using heroin.

Blood tests from the apparent PD victims came back negative for a panel of drugs, but did not examine all categories of drugs, just those known to contribute to motor symptoms (primarily neuroleptics, or antipsychotic medications). Perhaps a yet unknown strain of street drugs was the culprit, or even a contaminated batch of heroin. The fifth victim, the young mother labeled 'hysterical paralysis', and soon the sixth victim, the drug dealer, only confirmed this theory, as both had been using the same batch of heroin that was found in the previous victims' homes. Samples of the batch were collected and tested, and found to not contain any actual heroin at all. It was not even an opium derivative, as expected, but an entirely new compound of synthetic heroin.

An explanation for why the addicts had been using synthetic heroin lay in legal loopholes. While hard street drugs were and still are heavily regulated by the Drug Enforcement Agency (DEA) in the US, the law was specific about the chemical structures of those drugs, meaning that molecular changes to the compounds could bypass the regulations while having the same basic effect on the body (Henderson, 1988; Langston & Palfreman, 1995). Tracking the history of this particular designer drug revealed that the compound known as MPPP (an abbreviation for 1-methyl-4-phenyl-proprionoxypiperidine), created in the 1940s as the pain reliever Demerol, had been manipulated only six years before in 1976 into a designer drug five times more potent than the original compound. The drug's designer used his product reliably for months, until a hurried batch produced in him the exact symptoms that Langston was now seeing in his frozen addicts. Like his new addicts, the designer also responded well to L-Dopa therapy, but unfortunately continued to use recreational drugs and died of a cocaine overdose in 1978. Fortunately for Langston, though, the man's family had given consent to preserve and examine his brain post-mortem, and Langston was finally able to confirm pathologically through the near total obliteration of dopaminergic cells in the substantia nigra that this was indeed Parkinsonism. Now he simply had to figure out how to help his patients.

Dopamine is not able to pass through the blood-brain barrier, and therefore cannot be administered as a direct treatment option for Parkinson patients. L-Dopa, however, is actively transported into the brain and is then directly converted into dopamine, greatly increasing the availability of the critical neurotransmitter. Frozen and trapped patients react very well to L-Dopa, apparently waking up again and regaining almost all mobility. Yet the miracle drug is not without its faults, and its faults are many. Dopamine is also the primary neurotransmitter implicated in addiction, strengthening the connection between addictive drugs and degeneration of the dopamine system. Some patients therefore may experience a sort of 'rush' when the drug enters the system, the dosage of L-Dopa often needs to be increased as the disease progresses, much like tolerance to addictive drugs, and most will experience a sort of withdrawal, or 'wearing off' phenomena when the drug is evacuated from the system (Langston & Palfreman, 1995; Cenci & Lundblad, 2005).

The wearing off phenomena, in which Parkinsonism symptoms reappear between medication doses, is most evident shortly before the next dose of the short-lived medication is scheduled, may appear in multiple phases, and is magnified by stress or anxiety (Pfeiffer, 2005).

Aside from wearing off and a gradual loss of effectiveness, L-Dopa also produces significant and disturbing side effects. Those who take higher doses of the medication experience visual and tactile hallucinations, an artifact now well-documented in PD communities.[1] More than half of L-Dopa patients will at some point develop dyskinesias as well, or involuntary movements such as smooth, writhing motions or squirming in the face and limbs (Cenci & Lundblad, 2005; Friedman & Fernandez, 2005). Dyskinesias may be so disruptive that patients would rather stop medications and remain frozen, while others continue to experience the movements even after L-Dopa has been stopped. Because of this, supplemental medications are used to reduce the dose of L-Dopa needed for relief of symptoms, and in some cases, as a complete substitute for L-Dopa.

Other Therapeutic Options

The chemical at fault for damaging the brains of Langston's patients was MPTP, a toxic byproduct of the designer drug MPPP. Once through the blood brain barrier, MPTP is metabolized into MPP+ within astrocytes, and is then released and taken back up by dopaminergic neurons, where it interferes with mitochondrial function, functionally destroying the cell (Langston & Palfreman, 1995; Jackson-Lewis & Smeyne, 2005). Because monoamine-oxidase (MAO) enzymes play an active role in this metabolic chain, drugs that block these enzymes, such as the MAO-B inhibitor selegiline (trade name Deprenyl), may slow down the degeneration and even boost the effects of L-Dopa therapy. After going through rigorous testing, it was found that Deprenyl was able to successfully delay the onset of symptoms and slow disease progression by as much as 50% percent (Langston & Palfreman, 1995). Long-term follow-ups, however, have demonstrated that while these drugs may reduce the toxicity of MPTP in the substantia nigra, they may also shrink the overall size of the dopaminergic cells, and therefore may be toxic in their own right (Perlmutter & Tabbal, 2005).

Aside from MAO-inhibitors, Langston sought another avenue to restore the cells lost in his frozen addict patients: cell replacement. Now a rapidly growing field of study, stem cells can be obtained from many sources, but in the mid-1980s, the majority of what we knew about stem cells came from fetal sources, a hotly debated ethical argument (Langston & Palfreman, 1995). Traveling to Sweden for their procedures, two of the frozen addicts underwent bilateral fetal stem cell transplants in 1989. Their outcomes were a stunning success, restoring nearly all motor function, and the results were repeated with a third patient in 1994. However, due to the ethical debates surrounding the use of human fetal cells, as well as an *in vitro* concern of tumor growth from unregulated cell proliferation, modern transplant studies are exploring other cell types, including autologous transplants, or the grafting of cells from one area of the body to the brain. If the cells being transplanted are your own, then there is no risk of rejection of the graft, and the immune system does not need to be compromised to improve overall outcomes. Autologous grafts take time, however, and for those living with the effects of PD, time is of the essence.

An invasive, but highly effective, treatment is now available to those with advanced PD: deep brain stimulation (DBS). Using careful stereotactic surgery, thin metal electrodes are implanted deep within the brain in the subthalamic area or the globus pallidus, a major structure of the basal ganglia (Follett et al., 2010). The device is then connected to a stimulation device similar to a pacemaker, which delivers regular pulses of electrical stimulation, calibrated to the specific needs of the individual (Benabid et al., 2009). If set at the appropriate level of stimulation, DBS is able to reduce the resting tremors and rigidity of PD without producing the dyskinesias and emotional disturbances of drug-based therapies. Though highly effective, DBS is still not a perfect treatment option, as the surgery is invasive with some risk of complications, and hardware malfunction or breakdown can become an issue over time. Still, it remains a viable option for treating an otherwise baffling disease, and has since been expanded for use in treatment-resistant depression and obsessive-compulsive disorders.

Pathologies of Parkinsonism

The severe loss of dopaminergic cells in the substantia nigra may be the most prominent feature of PD pathology, but it is far from the only remarkable pathology, and it is also yet to be determined how and why such cell death occurs. Hypotheses over the years have included genetic factors, environmental toxins, and even head trauma, with none in complete agreement in regards to a single cause of Parkinsonism (Pfeiffer, 2005). In most cases, we can generally agree that PD is caused by a mix of the above factors, and rather than being a single, identifiable disease, may, in fact, be more of a spectrum disorder diagnosable by multi-system symptoms, and may even be related to other forms of motor system decline.

The Calne-Langston Hypothesis. In studying the frozen addicts, Langston and his team looked closer at the trademark pathology of PD: Cell death. They examined other heroin addicts who had used the bad batch containing MPTP but had not yet shown symptoms of PD, and found them to be at a higher risk for developing PD later in life compared to the general population (Langston & Palfreman, 1995). In the unaffected and unexposed population, cells in the nigrostriatal system (those connected to the substantia nigra and striatum of the basal ganglia) naturally die at a rate of 5–7 percent per decade. Combining these findings, Drs. Calne and Langston developed a new hypothesis: Exposure to toxic compounds earlier in life compounds with natural age-related cell death, leading to earlier onset of PD symptoms. For instance, if exposed to MPTP-contaminated heroin in one's 30s only once or twice, then natural cell death would lead to reaching the 80 percent cell death threshold of symptoms by the time one reaches their mid-60s.

This new hypothesis is certainly not perfect, as it does not account for aggressive and early-onset juvenile forms of PD, which show stronger familial connections and are more likely to be due to genetic factors. It does, however, fit more neatly with sporadic cases, which comprise the majority of PD cases. The toxin is not necessarily MPTP exactly, either. Rodent models utilize 6-hydroxydopamine (6-OHDA) to induce cell death, and rodent, primate, and human cases all show correlations to exposure to pesticides and herbicides such as paraquat and rotenone (Langston & Palfreman, 1995; Cenci & Lundblad, 2005; Pfeiffer, 2005; Gilbert, 2018). Genetics may make a person more or less susceptible to this form of damage, or may accelerate the natural degeneration of cells. There are other pathologies, though, that are not yet explained by this otherwise elegant hypothesis.

Lewy Body Dementias. While the discovery of MPTP led to a remarkable new laboratory model of advanced PD, the subjects with MPTP-induced damage were found to be missing the subcellular pathology of Lewy bodies (Perlmutter & Tabbal, 2005). The model does, however, show alterations to alpha-synuclein, the major protein found to be nitrated in Lewy bodies, indicating that this aggregating protein may be a precursor to the less-understood pathological marker of Lewy bodies (Jackson-Lewis & Smeyne, 2005). Found in brainstem areas as well as diffuse brain areas, Lewy bodies are small, dense inclusions connected to mitochondrial dysfunction and breakdown of protein degradation pathways, and a potential factor in cell death (Beyer et al., 2009). In PD cases, Lewy bodies form deep in the brainstem and in the olfactory system, the region that controls smell perception,[2] and later spreads to the basal ganglia, limbic system, and eventually cortex.

Lewy bodies are also the major pathology associated with a similar, but unique form of dementia, known either as dementia with Lewy bodies (DLB) or Lewy body dementia (LBD) depending on the spectrum of symptoms presented. Comparatively lesser-known, LBD may be misdiagnosed as PD if its most prominent symptoms are motor, or if the patient fails to report emotional and cognitive symptoms for whatever reasons, be they memory loss or fear. Such a misdiagnosis even happened to beloved comedian Robin Williams, who was experiencing severe anxiety and autonomic symptoms on top of motor stiffness and tremor, but chose not to report his hallucinations (Williams, 2016). And while there is not currently an effective therapy available for people with LBD, it is still important to delineate the diseases from one another, as the side effects of PD treatments may aggravate LBD symptoms and worsen the person's condition. Therefore, we must continue to encourage communication in both directions of the patient–doctor relationship, so that we can reduce such debilitating errors in the future.

Future Directions

Designer drugs have continued to be a problem in modern society since the days of the bad batch of synthetic heroin. Whenever there are regulations in place, there will also be people to find loopholes around those regulations. For instance, aside from the synthetic heroin that produced neurotoxic MPTP, another narcotic derived from fentanyl, nicknamed 'China White', was produced and spread through California suburbs in the late 1970s, and has been further manipulated into other, technically legal forms since then (Henderson, 1988). In the twenty-first century, phencyclidine (PCP, or 'Angel Dust') further damaged the dopamine as well as norepinephrine systems (Bey & Patel, 2007), and yet another opiate-derivative called 'krokodil' began to rot and decay the flesh of its still-living victims (Haskin et al., 2016). This list does not yet include the effects of synthetic cathinones like 'bath salts', which are chemically similar to amphetamines, and which have been the topic of a 'Florida Man' newspaper headline involving cannibalism (ABC, 2012). Aside from the physical and societal threats that these customized drugs pose, we must also consider the role that these play in the health of our brains.

Far from suggesting a completely drug-free society, more research is targeting the development of neuroprotective drugs for at-risk individuals. For instance, in recovering addicts who had been exposed to neurotoxic compounds, perhaps treatment with MAO-B inhibitors can protect their substantia nigra from excess degeneration. In those who have already developed symptoms of PD, perhaps DBS therapy can help to maintain the existing cells and pathways that yet survive, limiting the progression of the disease. In genetic forms of PD, exploration into epigenetics, or how dormant genes become activated or inactivated, can prevent the disease state from taking root in the first place. In any path, though, we must rely on one another and always seek to help others.

Notes

1 Parkinsonism and schizophrenia have an unusual connection, sometimes considered to be on opposite ends of a spectrum. When there are abnormally high levels of dopamine in the frontal lobe, schizophrenia symptoms manifest. When dopamine is reduced by antipsychotic medications, Parkinsonism symptoms manifest. When low dopamine levels in PD are increased by L-Dopa, psychotic symptoms manifest.
2 Interestingly, an early and often disregarded symptom of many forms of dementia is a loss of the sense of smell, or Anosmia. Since the loss is also associated with other factors like smoking and allergies, it is typically ignored and only recognized later when more prominent symptoms have appeared.

Chapter 11

'The One True Superman'

Christopher Reeve's Steps
toward Hope

You'll Believe a Man Can Fly

First hitting shelves in 1938, the iconic red, yellow, and blue uniform of one of the most well-known comic book heroes is now synonymous with justice and good. Superman is credited with initiating the superhero genre, and inspires an unending number of movies, television shows, and books. The character became especially popular when the scope of TV and movies expanded after WWII and was further immortalized on the silver screen in 1978 by Julliard alumni Christopher Reeve. Reeve became his role, remaining a standard for successive Supermen to live up to. But it would be his actions post-Superman that would truly cement his name in the list of those standing for justice as well as kindness and morality.

An accomplished equestrian, Reeve took part in a competition in Virginia in 1995. He was prepared well, wearing a helmet and vest to protect himself from injury. He appeared to do everything right. While running a course of 18 obstacles, he and his mount cleared the first two easily, but the horse stopped suddenly at the third obstacle, a three-foot high log-jump (Cimons, 1995). The momentum threw Reeve forward over the front of the horse and onto the ground, where he landed on his head. Though his head was protected by the helmet, his neck was not. The top two cervical vertebrae of his spine, known as C1 and C2, were broken.

The spinal column is separated into four sections: Cervical, comprising the neck down to the top of the shoulders; thoracic, along the ribcage; lumbar, between the ribs and hips[1]; and sacral, from the hips to the tailbone. Reeve's injury was at the very top of the cervical region, directly adjacent to the skull and brainstem, the latter of which controls major organ functions such as breathing and heart rate. Also known as a 'hangman's fracture' due to its similarity to those hanged by the neck, C1 injuries have a high fatality rate, making Reeve's condition that much more serious. He was rushed to emergency care, and while expressing initial confusion as to why he was in the hospital, his cognitive state was overall intact. The high-level injury did affect his lung function, necessitating the use of a ventilator and surgery to stabilize the fractured bones, now common practice to relieve pressure on the spinal cord and prevent fragments of bone from lacerating the cord and thereby worsening the injury. His situation was grim, but doctors, as well as friends[2] and family members, were hopeful that there would still be room for recovery despite the long-held concept that the brain and spinal cord were not capable of regeneration. Reeve would be among a long list of those to prove that the archaic idea was, in fact, total bunk.

Ultimately, Reeve would be left with an almost total loss of mobility and sensation below the neck. Clinically, this is referred to as a 'complete' injury, with 'incomplete' injuries being those that spare some degree of sensation or partial movement. The definitions of complete/incomplete are now changing, however, to include more biochemical and physiological characteristics based on findings that most human spinal cord injuries still maintain small amounts of tissue that traverse the injury site, and that truly complete injuries are relatively rare (Norenberg et al., 2004). Typically, the more 'sparing' of tissue, or undamaged tissue left after the injury, the greater the prognosis for recovery of function. In animal models, as little as 5–10 percent spared tissue around the site of the injury is needed to promote significant recovery (Mautes et al., 2000). Having a diagnosis of 'complete' with an estimate of 0 percent spared tissue meant that Reeve's prognosis was very grim. He was not one to take this news lying down, though.

While relying on a ventilator for the remainder of his life, Reeve never gave up hope, and continued to fight for recovery in a world so pessimistic about spinal cord injuries (SCI). As the new face of the SCI community, Reeve and his wife, Dana, began the Christopher Reeve Foundation (later changed to the Christopher & Dana Reeve Foundation in recognition of her contributions as well), dedicated to supporting research endeavors, providing information and help to those living with

SCI, and advocating for the rights of the disabled (CDRF, 2019). Under his and his family's advocacy efforts, a 1999 bill was passed to allow people with disabilities to work (thereby also boosting mental health) without losing disability benefits, the NIH research budget more than doubled in only five years, and millions now had access to free resources and advice to help get through what would likely be the most difficult time of their lives. He continued to act and wrote two memoirs after his injury, earning multiple awards, including in recognition of his human rights efforts.

Life expectancy after sustaining a severe SCI is significantly lower than uninjured or 'minor' injured individuals. And, like many other individuals affected by the chronic effects of SCI, Reeve experienced a myriad of secondary effects, eventually succumbing to a severe infection and passing away in 2004, just nine years after his injury. While being treated for a pressure sore that had become infected, an all too common occurrence in those with SCIs, Reeve's body was unable to fight it any longer, and he suffered cardiac arrest before slipping into a coma. His wife, Dana, would follow him two years later. The Reeve children, Matthew, Alexandra, and Will, continue to actively participate in their parents' efforts with the foundation, keeping up the heroic, life-changing outreach and research support that benefits so many SCI victims and their families.

The Unexpected Effects

Commonly, when people hear the term spinal cord injury, the first thing that comes to mind is the loss of movement and sensation at and below the level of the injury. For example, an injury at the mid to low thoracic level (chest) would not affect the arms, but would affect the lower torso and legs. However, there are more systems involved in these bodily areas than just the sensorimotor pathways. Many individuals affected by SCI even cite that the secondary effects of their injuries are more aggravating than the loss of mobility. As with Reeve, high level cervical injuries compromise lung function and regular breathing, but also heart rate and blood pressure, digestion, bowel and bladder function, thermoregulation, and the immune system. While entire volumes of textbooks can be dedicated to these complications, here we will focus on three common complaints.

Autonomic Dysfunction. The autonomic nervous system in the peripheral nervous system regulates vital organ systems like the heart and lungs, as well as the other major organs and digestive system. Post-injury, there is a high risk of a condition known as autonomic dysreflexia, in which the system essentially goes into panic mode. Heart rate and blood pressure may temporarily rise dangerously high, and if left unattended or unidentified may be fatal. Symptoms can include otherwise innocuous signs like headaches, anxiety, and nasal congestion, making it crucial for medical professionals to be trained in identifying an episode (Krassioukov et al., 2009). Autonomic dysreflexia is more common in those whose injuries are at or above T6 (the sixth thoracic vertebrae) and the risk further increases for those with higher and more complete injuries. Fortunately, when we are prepared to deal with dysreflexia episodes, the condition is readily treatable and even preventable. For many people with SCI, bladder irritation is a major trigger, along with other noxious stimuli[3] below the site of injury, so treating bladder and bowel issues can prevent episodes from happening. Prolonged episodes can be treated with acute antihypertensive medications, but consistent use of these drugs is not recommended, as they can lead to the counter-response of severely decreased blood pressure.

Bladder and Bowel Function. While nobody likes to talk about what comes out of the far end of the digestive system, it is, nonetheless, a necessary part of life, and one that those living with SCI are all too aware of. The spinal cord supplies communication between the brain and body for all systems, including digestion, and when damaged,[4] leads to significant compromises to the bladder and bowels. Clinically referred to as neurogenic bladder and neurogenic bowel, effects include incontinence and/or inability to void (Benevento & Sipski, 2002), and are listed among the top frustrations of people with SCI, often rating higher than the loss of mobility. When at all possible, the best treatment and management plans consider the dignity of the person affected, and allow them to maintain control of their own regimen. Most people will choose either indwelling or intermittent catheterization for bladder function, and a combination of over-the-counter treatments and digital stimulation for bowel evacuation. Ironically, bladder regimens often recommend limiting fluid intake to prevent excess pressure (and inducing an autonomic dysreflexia episode), while bowel regimens suggest increasing water intake. As with other conditions, it is encouraged that the individual affected learns their own needs and that caregivers who assist these individuals listen and provide care according to the unique situation.

Immune System. While Reeve's official cause of death was cardiac arrest, those in the SCI community highlight the point that he was being treated for an infection at the time of the attack, which had arisen from a pressure sore. Both pressure sores and infections are an all too common occurrence for people with SCI due to the combination of restricted mobility and a weakened immune system. Reductions in immune function are so common with any injury to the central nervous system that it is sometimes referred to as CNS injury-induced immunodepression, or CIDS (Meisel et al., 2005). In SCI, immunodepression is so severe that an estimated 50% of post-SCI deaths are related to infections such as pneumonia and septicemia, which is likely the sort that took hold of Christopher Reeve. Entire schools of science are determined to identify the cause of immunodepression, though individuals affected would rather know how to manage the condition and reduce the damage to quality of life. Anti-inflammatories are often recommended to treat active insults to the system, and immunomodulators are being tested for efficacy, while antibiotics can of course be given when appropriate. As in many other situations, prevention is best. But when prevention is not a viable option, such as when in a hospital setting or participating in normal social activities, understanding of the condition and proper care and exercise can reduce how taxed the already strained immune system is.

Neuropathic Pain. With the great possibilities of regeneration that are being discovered, an unfortunate side effect was sure to follow. In the case of SCI, it is neuropathic pain. Thought to arise from aberrant or incorrect reconnections in the spinal circuitry, this pain is severe, often chronic, and does not respond to typical analgesic treatments. Injuries can also initiate or exacerbate existing pain disorders such as trigeminal neuralgia, a pain disorder in cranial nerve V that is reported to feel like simultaneous stabbing and burning throughout the face, and is nicknamed a type of 'suicide pain' (Anonymous, 2019). Unsurprisingly, such pain is extremely disruptive to quality of life as well as recovery, and so active research efforts are attempting to identify potential targets for treatments. Tricyclic antidepressants and anticonvulsant medications both have some success in reducing the severity of pain, though they should be tested and added/removed based on the individuals' needs. On an experimental basis, the otherwise lauded brain-derived neurotrophic factor (BDNF), known for its ability to promote cell health and regrowth, has now been implicated in post-SCI neuropathic pain (Matyas et al., 2017a). Excessive level of astrocytes in the glial scar express a subtype of receptor for BDNF known as TrkB.T1, which is significantly upregulated in the presence of painful hypersensitivity. Microchemical techniques utilizing interleukins and micro-RNAs are being tested in animal subjects with some success (Sabirzhanov et al., 2019), though this is still in early stages of testing. Still, the idea provides the hope of relief for thousands currently living with severe daily pain.

Potential Therapies

As more people than ever are surviving their injuries, so too is there a greater need for therapies to improve day-to-day function, as well as provide hope and support as people push toward recovery. Many options are currently available, and new and exciting avenues are becoming available every day. It is first and foremost important to consider the individual's needs when designing a treatment plan so that no unnecessary medications are given, and no helpful options are disregarded.

Anti-inflammatories and Decompression. As with brain injuries, spinal injuries carry a high likelihood of inflammation and swelling as a direct result of the injury. Emergency treatments therefore have to consider this when tending to an injured patient. Common practice in the past has been administration of the anti-inflammatory steroid methylprednisolone, which can be effective if administered within eight hours of the injury (Rosenzweig & McDonald, 2004). However, it is ineffective beyond this point, and may generate more side effects than benefits, so its use should be carefully considered based on individual needs.

Surgical decompression is another often selected option to reduce intraspinal pressure. In the presence of bone fractures, there is a risk that pieces may split off and lacerate the cord. In absence of fractures, the intact bone does not expand as the cord swells, necessitating the spinal counterpart to a craniotomy: The removal of bone to reduce pressure on the CNS tissue. This can include laminectomy, or removal of the spinal lamina (between the projections of the vertebrae), or replacement of the fragmented vertebrae with cadaver tissues. Stabilization with hardware is then placed to support the spine's structure and improve functional outcomes (Ojo et al., 2017).

While many people with SCI pursue massage to stimulate the muscle systems and relieve aches, due to the structural changes to the spine following decompression surgeries, frequenting chiropractors or massage therapists who have not had formal experience with intravertebral hardware is not recommended. Training is available, though, to teach specialists the proper way to manage hardware and avoid harming or aggravating the client's injuries, allowing many access to the advantages of massage without the risk of interfering with recovery progress.

Exercise Therapy. Seldom is there a condition where it would not be recommended to 'eat well and exercise', and SCI is no exception. While exercise can certainly be difficult when there is a significant loss of motor control, it is not impossible, and should be employed whenever possible. Like the standard 'use it or lose it' law, muscles are susceptible to atrophy after SCI due to lack of use, and exercise can help to prevent this muscle wasting. Animal experimentation has utilized motorized equipment to simulate the movements required for exercise like bicycling, which subsequently improved voluntary control of these muscle groups and increased neuroregeneration[5] (Houle & Cote, 2013). Human counterparts to this are readily available in rehabilitation centers as well as for in-home use, such as the NuStep, a recumbent bike which can be operated using the arms. Simply getting the body moving can help relieve muscle pain and improve one's mood state, while simultaneously boosting regeneration in the nervous system.

Stem Cell Transplantation. Christopher Reeve was himself a strong supporter of stem cell research, which has demonstrated increasingly exciting results in improving neuroregeneration. Despite the long-held reputation of stem cells being ethically controversial, very few scientific groups still utilize fetal stem cells, instead opting for adult-source stem cells that show more benefits with lower risks of tumor growth. Adult stem cells can be found in a myriad of body regions, and depending on the source and time of cell, can have different benefits. For example, olfactory ensheathing cells obtained from the nasal region may promote remyelination and signaling (Tello Velasquez et al., 2015), neural precursor cells collected from the subventricular zone or other regions of the CNS can mature into new neurons as well as other glial cells, directly replacing the lost tissues (Nishimura et al., 2013), and mesenchymal cells harvested from bone marrow, fat, or blood can modulate the immune response and promote recovery by allowing the body to repair itself with less interference (Matyas et al., 2017b; Stewart et al., 2017). Many of these cells can further be collected from one's own body, called an autologous transplant, eliminating both the need for tissue donors and the risk of transplant rejection.

Electrical Stimulation and Robotics. In a great union between science and engineering, the field of biomedical engineering has brought tremendous prospects and optimism to neurotrauma victims. Recent advancements have included bioelectronic implants, thin membranes that provide electrical stimulation directly to the spinal cord below the site of injury to retrain the lower spine to respond as it used to, and robotic exoskeletons, computerized braces that respond to subtle body movements to promote movement and walking, even for those with severe injuries.

Bioelectronic implants have their roots in one of the main rules of neurodevelopment, Hebb's law: Neurons that fire together wire together. The principle states that the more frequently two neurons communicate with one another, the stronger the connection between them, so the more that circuit is used, the more easily it works. Biomechanically, it is much like muscle training in exercise. When first trying a new pattern of exercise (or any task really), it may be difficult. But the more that pattern is practiced, the easier it becomes, and the faster we can execute it. With bioelectronic implants, an array of electrodes is implanted over the center of the dura of the spinal cord, typically in the lumbar to sacral regions (but potentially in the brain as well, depending on one's needs), and connected to a wireless control device to deliver constant pulses of electrical stimulation when activated (Harkema et al., 2011; Cho et al., 2019). Training is necessary, but there has been such success that individuals who received these implants have been able to recover not only mobility years after their injuries, but also regained bowel and bladder function, and the confidence that comes with both (Harkema et al., 2011).

Another potential engineering option is exoskeletons, which are specially designed to respond to the individual's muscle groups and subtle movements to facilitate natural movement and gait. Equipment is still extremely expensive, and potentially out of reach for the majority of the SCI community as of 2020, but there is no argument that exoskeleton technology has dramatic benefits in cardiovascular health, physical activity, and mental health (Gorgey, 2018). Potential complications of using the devices could include risk of skin breakdown from irritation at the contact points of the device, risk of bone fracture for those with decreased bone density, and the devices are currently limited to use by individuals within a certain weight or size and injury level. The companies that manufacture the devices are already actively working to resolve these issues, though, and one in particular, ReWalk, is able to be used by individuals with little to no function in the lower limbs (Guanziroli et al., 2019). The device detects tilting movements in the torso and changes to the center of gravity, as well as elbow movements in the crutches that assist with balance. To see the device in use, however, an even more amazing feature is the smile that comes across the face of someone who had previously been told they would never walk again as they stand and walk across a room. In this regard, the hope that this new technology provides is priceless, and validates every dollar that went into its production.

Future Research

We've made amazing strides in the past few years alone when it comes to recovery from SCI, and we have the support of Christopher Reeve and his family to thank for many of those accomplishments, though we still have a distance to go. Availability of innovative new therapies is out of reach for most of the SCI community due to cost and insurance limitations, and complications like pain and infections are an ongoing impediment to rehabilitation. In clinical settings, many are still stuck in the pages of outdated textbooks and the idea that recovery is never possible, indicating that communication among the sciences is critically needed. Going forward from here, we can look forward to a hopeful new future with new developments in stem cell transplantation and bioelectronics, which are sure to keep going forward at a rate faster than a speeding bullet.

Notes

1 This is the section that curves inward, known as lordosis (the thoracic area curves outwards in kurtosis). The inward curvature is healthy

for the human spine and upright posture, which is the major goal of furniture that features 'lumbar support'. While it may feel awkward to use lumbar support at first, this may even be helpful to prevent issues with the intervertebral discs, a common issue associated with lower back pain in adults.

2 Robin Williams was a very close friend of Reeve's, having been his roommate at Julliard. He was reportedly the first person able to make Reeve smile and laugh after the accident, adding a little light of cheer and hope to an otherwise depressing situation.

3 This can include things as dramatic as surgical or office procedures, or things as harmless as constrictive clothing. Those who have experienced a single episode are more likely to understand their own triggers, and are encouraged to communicate with doctors and caregivers to further decrease risk of additional episodes.

4 Damage to any region of the spinal cord can disrupt bowel and bladder function, as many of the spinal circuits that control these systems are located in the sacral cord near the tailbone. The same is true for sexual function, which is similarly avoided in discussion but is disrupted by spinal injuries.

5 The benefits of exercise have been so significant in promoting recovery that common experimental practice is to restrict exercise in animals. An animal allowed more exercise recovers so well that it is no longer clear whether the improvements are due to the experiment or the exercise. Unfortunately, it does not have as significant an effect in humans, so the current state of exercise therapy is as a standard rehabilitation technique to be used as a combinatory approach, or to do at the same time as other treatments.

Chapter 12

'A Stream of Water is Endlessly Beautiful'

Jason Padgett and Acquired Savant Syndrome

Untapped Potential Now Tapped

In the spring of 2016, the National Neurotrauma Society held its annual conference in Louisville, Kentucky. Its presidential lecture took place in an elegant art studio packed full of eager and excited young neuroscientists. So, when the keynote speaker took the stage, all ears were open. An apparently shy man with kind eyes stepped up to the mic to tell his story; one full of both physical and emotional trauma; one of both setbacks and of recovery; and altogether full of hope. What was to follow the speech was surely a nightmare to its deliverer: a barrage of questions from a mob of strangers eager to know the most intimate details of the story. And yet, in spite of the overwhelming nature of the situation, Jason Padgett remained an open book.

Padgett's journey through neurotrauma began in 2002, when a violent mugging changed his life forever. Self-described as a 'mediocre at best' student during his youth, he would unknowingly be launched into the world of genius and mathematical sciences. One September night, he met friends at a karaoke bar to enjoy a fun night out. He was the designated driver, a choice that may have ultimately improved his outcome. However, a few other bar patrons were not so sober. After spotting some cash in his wallet when paying for a soda at the bar, Padgett was ambushed just outside the door, first being beaten on the right side of his head behind the ear, which drove him to the floor and set off immediate visual and auditory effects (a white flash of light and a loud, low, piano-like sound) (Padgett & Seaberg, 2014). He tried to stand, but was struck again from the other side, then again, and again. Eventually, the barrage ended when the two men rifled through his pockets and made off with his leather jacket, but not the cash that had incited the attack. Calling out for help, the bar employees refused, but his panicked friend went with him to the nearest hospital. Among his other myriad of physical injuries, he was diagnosed as having a 'profound concussion' and sent home. His attackers would never be brought to justice.

The visual effects of the attack began immediately. Aside from the initial flash of white light, moving items appeared to leave colorful trails, geometric patterns overlaid everything in sight, and movement appeared choppy instead of fluid, an artifact known as akinetopsia.[1] These were attributed to the concussion with the hopes that they would resolve on their own, and in the meantime, the images Padgett was seeing were quite beautiful. A stream of water from the faucet produced perpendicular lines that spread over the entire room. Driving was full of whole new sets of distractions as light played off of surfaces. Now seen as a blessing in disguise, this new visual world would not fade through his course of recovery, but was here to stay, and brought along several other not-so-beautiful side effects.

Violent assaults typically leave significant emotional scars, and many victims are understandably left with post-traumatic stress disorder (PTSD). In this situation, where Padgett had been attacked in a familiar place in his own neighborhood, nobody would be surprised to learn that he, too, would develop PTSD. Often comorbid with, or occurring at the same time as other types of anxiety disorders, Padgett would also be subject to obsessive-compulsive disorder (OCD) and agoraphobia, finding himself counting and repeating certain tasks (with particular attention to prime numbers), and barricading himself within his home with sheets nailed over the windows. Isolation in cases of agoraphobia is frequently seen as preferable to the anxiety and panic attacks that accompany leaving one's home or neighborhood. And while Padgett did remain at home for a couple of years after the attack, he was able to recognize the symptoms, reading and educating himself on the condition, and venturing out late at night for groceries and other essentials (Padgett & Seaberg, 2014). At the same time, he began to read up on other experiences, finally identifying an explanation for the visual kaleidoscope he had been seeing since that fateful night.

Synesthesia (or synaesthesia) is known essentially as a blending of the senses, or a cross-wiring between the five main human senses. By those unfamiliar with the phenomenon, an explanation is often met with comments like 'you can't hear colors, that's ridiculous'. And while most people cannot hear colors, there are many people who can, as well as others who can taste sounds or images, see specific colors when looking at letters or numbers, and feel touch when others are touched (Ramachandran & Hubbard, 2003; Hubbard & Ramachandran, 2005; Ward et al., 2018). In Jason Padgett's case, he is able to see math. Sometime after he began to delve into scientific papers and shows, he came across Dr. Treffert, a scientist and fellow synesthete out of Wisconsin, whose papers and presentations introduced him to an entire world of people just like him. And while it would be a while longer before getting an official diagnosis, Padgett fit the bill perfectly.

Knowing now that what he was seeing was, in fact, fractals and geometrical patterns, Padgett began to draw what he was seeing, producing detailed and beautiful illustrations. He pushed himself to leave his solitary confinement and return to school, eventually being recognized for his newfound talent and being additionally identified as having acquired savant syndrome, or a remarkably high level of talent in a specific topic; in his case, mathematics. Anxiety and OCD were still a significant problem, but he states that the beauty of his synesthetic world was worth the payoff. To share such images with everyone, he began to attend conferences such as the National Neurotrauma Society meeting, sharing his story and his illustrations. Prints of his stunning illustrations are available online at Jason-Padgett.pixels.com, or at FineArtAmerica.com/Profiles/Jason-Padgett, including the Quantum Nautilus, a superimposition of triangles over the spiral shape of a nautilus shell (Figure 12.1).

The Unexpected Effects

This chapter differs from others in that we are *not* going to be discussing disabilities or deficits that developed as a result of the initial injury. Instead, this chapter focuses on newly developed abilities and altered perceptions. Individuals living with the following abilities are not suffering due to their differences; they simply see the world differently than others, leading to a major terminology change in the field of neuroscience: Neurotypical as opposed to healthy or unaffected individuals. If you would like

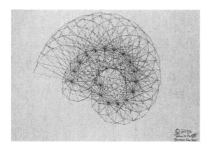

Figure 12.1 Thumbnail copy of 'The Quantum Nautilus' by Jason Padgett. Following his head injury and subsequent development of mathematical synesthesia, Padgett began to draw what he was able to see in everyday life. The Quantum Nautilus in particular is made entirely out of right triangles of varying sizes. This image is reprinted with permissions from Mr. Jason Padgett, and prints of this and other pieces can be purchased through his website and through Fine Art America.

to read more about his personal story and details on his management of PTSD and other anxieties, Padgett has published a book of his own entitled *Struck by Genius*, and a film adaptation is now in the works.

Synesthesia. Roughly translated as a sync in sensations, synesthesia is thought to be due to extra connections or cross-connectivity in the brain compared to neurotypical individuals. In order to be confirmed as a synesthete, or a person with synesthesia, the sensations, be they visual, auditory, or tactile, must be automatic and involuntary, and must be consistent from test to retest (Hubbard & Ramachandran, 2005; Neufeld et al., 2013; Padgett & Seaberg, 2014). The sensations are not the same as metaphors, such as common idioms like 'red in the face' or 'a sharp taste' (Ramachandran & Hubbard, 2003), though it is possible to have more associative forms where the individual does not necessarily *see* the colors,[2] but simply knows that the number five, for instance, is a specific shade of dark red (Hubbard & Ramachandran, 2005). The most common form of synesthesia is grapheme-color synesthesia, or the perception of numbers and letters/words as specific colors. The colors may be somewhat different from person to person, but are always consistent within an individual. Padgett's particular form of mathematical synesthesia is quite rare, in that he is the only known and documented case so far. Rather than seeing colors assigned to numbers, he sees the geometrical figures and fractals that comprise the world around us on a sub-molecular level. Compared to theoretical images such as the Mandelbrot set, he states that his vision matches perfectly. This remarkable ability contributed quite a bit to another that he developed simultaneously: Savant syndrome.

Acquired Savant Syndrome. Savantism refers to a high level of ability in specific areas, called an 'island of genius', typically occurring in individuals with a disability in other areas, though the disability is not necessarily a requirement for a confirmed identification of savantism (Treffert, 2009). Traditionally, savant syndrome is associated with mental deficits such as those who are developmentally delayed. The popular movie *Rain Man* in 1988 depicted real life savant Kim Peek who, while significantly impaired intellectually and socially, possessed a vast encyclopedic knowledge and rapid reading and memorization level that earned him the title 'mega-savant' (Treffert, 2009; Padgett & Seaberg, 2014). Eventually it was separated out as an ability not isolated to the mentally disabled, and the term 'idiot savant' evolved into 'autistic savant', though this is still a gross misnomer. An early estimate stated that about 10 percent of those on the autism spectrum[3] were also savants, and less than half of all savants happened to be on the autism spectrum (Treffert, 1999). Today it is known that savantism may be a developmental difference or an acquired skill after head trauma, as in Padgett's case.

There are several connections between savantism and synesthesia. One of the identifying characteristics of savantism is a massive, highly detailed memory (Treffert, 2009; Neufeld et al., 2013). A potential explanation of the strong memory system in savants may be the presence of unidentified synesthesia, an idea supported by Luria's famous patient, S., who was found to have as many as five different modalities of sensory synesthesia (Padgett & Seaberg, 2014). Other explanations have included genetic factors, as well as the suggestion that synesthesia may be more common in autism, though the exact reason for the connection is yet unknown. Theoretically, both abilities may be the result of either hyper-connectivity in the brain through differential development, or the release of a sort of 'filter' by damage to the brain's inhibitory areas.

Vicariation and compensatory mechanisms are key terms in neuroplasticity, or the study of how the brain changes over time. Vicariation refers to the ability of surviving brain areas to sort of pick up the slack for areas that are damaged, such as shifting control of the leg to a nearby area after a stroke, while other compensatory mechanisms can include increased sensitivity or neural activation in other, uninjured areas. For Jason Padgett, a theoretical explanation of his newfound abilities is that the damage to his brain, which occurred first at the right parietal lobe, the 'perception center' of the brain, led to a disinhibition of the more calculating left hemisphere, which then compensated by increasing its activity levels (Padgett & Seaberg, 2014). The idea has led to a lot of chatter in academic circles as to whether everybody is capable of savant-level skills, but that the neurotypical brain inhibits these abilities in favor of being well rounded. However, when asked if an acute trauma may potentially release these hidden abilities, Padgett stated that he would not recommend it (Padgett, 2016).

Hyper-Empathy. While Padgett has considered the idea, he expresses that he would not trade his new abilities to return to the way life was. His world is beautiful, and while he does struggle with multiple forms of anxiety, some of these can be seen as yet another added benefit, such as hyper-empathy. Though highly distressful in many situations (imagine feeling intense sadness when seeing another person weep), people who rate high in empathy are often seen as kind and caring individuals, and form deep emotional connections to others. Empathy as a human emotion has been heavily studied but poorly understood overall, but new findings have suggested the idea that it may be related to yet another form of synesthesia, known as mirror-touch synesthesia. In typical human empathy, we see another person express sadness, anger, or fear, and we feel a tinge of it ourselves. We even mimic the other person's facial expressions unconsciously, activating a special system called the Mirror Neuron System[4] (Bons et al., 2013). In hyper-empathy, though, this system kicks into overdrive, leading to stronger and more personal emotions in response to others' emotional expressions. The suggested connection to synesthetes, mirror-touch synesthesia, involves the perception of physical sensations when viewing someone else being touched. The effect has been recorded as boosting a person's ability to accurately read facial expressions, as well as increased emotional empathy, or feeling the emotion that is being observed (Ward et al., 2018). Though it can be argued that this form of synesthesia is more of an alternate form of empathy than a type of hyper-empathy, those living with it would surely like the idea to be explored in more depth.

Future Research

For as long as we can tell, people have been searching for ways to release their maximum potential and reveal hidden skills or talents. Experiments on nootropics, or drugs that can boost intelligence, have all fallen flat and gone the way of pseudoscience and snake-oil. But now evidence finally exists to say that there may be secret abilities buried in the human brain after all in the form of synesthesia. However, if the way to tap into these abilities is to be bashed around the head, then certainly we are far away from an applied method for releasing the abilities. Cases like Padgett's and his peers have certainly given us great insight into a world that others cannot see, and will continue to encourage people to express and talk about being able to sense multiple modalities at once without being labeled 'crazy'. Further connections between synesthesia and savantism provide well-supported evidence of both rare phenomena.

As always, the key to advancing research on synesthesia and savantism is communication. We now have an academically inviting atmosphere in which Padgett and his peers can talk about their experiences without fear of judgment. Because of this, fewer people are resisting the idea of cross-sensory perceptions, and more are working on determining the neural circuits involved in how these super-abilities work. We still have a long way to go in answering the great question of how to improve our own intelligence, but we are at least going in the right direction by admitting that we have more to learn.

Additional Note

Despite the discussion here of connections to the autism spectrum, it must be made known that autism *cannot* be acquired, though it is not necessarily a disability either. More often, accompanying sensory processing disorder (SPD) is more disruptive to the individual than differences in social interaction, and should be treated as a separate condition. For instance, people on the autism spectrum have been cited as having lower empathy than neurotypical individuals, though some speculate that it is only motor and cognitive empathy that is affected, while emotional empathy is heightened, potentially further explaining feeling discomforted and overwhelmed by eye contact with others. In SPD, certain senses become magnified, and the sensory threshold is lowered, making a person easily overwhelmed or susceptible to perceived pain than neurotypical people. Considering the existing literature on synesthesia, it is not unreasonable to speculate that eye contact and its connection to empathy may be a sort of synesthetic SPD in people on the autism spectrum, though this has yet to be tested and verified.

Notes

1 Akinetopsia translates directly into 'no movement vision', and exists on a spectrum of severity, with some cases being episodic or temporary. Some individuals with severe akinetopsia cannot see cars move or liquid pouring. The car simply transports from one position to another, and empty mugs are suddenly filled to overflowing.

2 Those who perceive the merged sensation in their environment are referred to as 'projectors', while those who cannot explain, but know in their mind's eye are called 'associators'. These may have different neurological pathways, but are still being explored.

3 Note also that the 'disorder' designation has been removed from the autism spectrum, as the state of being autistic is no longer seen as a disability. It is more likely to be referred to as a 'disorder of the observer', wherein the individual affected is not bothered or harmed by the behaviors displayed, but that others are. Instead, it is specified that there may be maladaptive behaviors present, but these are more likely to be comorbidities than defining features.

4 Mirror neurons have been identified while learning and imitating new tasks during observational learning, and are especially prominent in children. Therefore, the imitation of others and perhaps empathy itself is hard-wired into us.

Chapter 13

'Man Bites Dog'

How Rabies Encephalitis May Someday Be Curable

Just One Bite

It's a classic horror story trope: After being bitten by a vicious canine, a man begins to change. At first, nothing happens. But soon, anxiety, confusion, and aggression appear. In the throes of the curse, he would harm his own best friend. It is also a story rooted in truth. While the classic werewolf mythos and literal transformation into a canine-like creature are of course, fantasy, the mental effects of the legend may be based closely on the rabies virus. Records of rabies infections or rabies-like symptoms go back over 4000 years, potentially originating in the Middle East and spreading worldwide (Tarantola, 2017).

The disease traditionally was associated with bites from dogs, which have been our companions for longer than written records can specify. After a bite from a dog, sufferers would typically have a delay of symptoms for weeks to years at a time, eventually spreading from the initial injury to the nerves, onward into the spinal cord, and ending in the brain (Susilawathi et al., 2012). Until this point, there is an overall absence of symptoms other than typical irritation from the bite or scratch, and beyond this point, no treatment methods are effective at delaying mortality. When symptoms finally appear, they commonly include agitation and confusion, paralysis, excessive salivation, difficulty swallowing, psychotic-like features such as hallucinations and hydrophobia (an irrational fear of water), and other equally painful symptoms. The onset of neurological symptoms is, therefore, considered to be a 'point of no return' for infection with the rabies virus. All traditional attempts at treating it were more distressing than the symptoms themselves. Most focused on treating the initial bite before symptoms appeared, including cauterizing the wounds, faith-based or mystical approaches, or topical remedies, the latter of which may include a 'hair of the dog that bit you', originating the still-common idiom. The most humane option for centuries was euthanasia, often by smothering the affected person to death between mattresses. The disease was so aggressively fatal that one military general attempted to weaponize it in the seventeenth century by filling hollow ammunition shells with contaminated dog saliva.[1] Unfortunately, it remains as fatal now as it was hundreds of years ago.

Eventually, a vaccine was developed and refined over time, but these to date are only effective before the onset of symptoms, which is then labeled clinical rabies (Hattwick et al., 1972; Willoughby et al., 2005; CDC, 2009; Susilawathi et al., 2012; Tarantola, 2017). Preventative vaccines administered to pets dramatically reduced the incidence rates in humans, though there has been limited success with this type of vaccines in humans. Post-exposure prophylaxis is fortunately very successful, having been developed and tested in the late nineteenth century, and now has a nearly 100 percent success rate when administered immediately after exposure (Jackson et al., 2003; Tarantola, 2017). Availability, though, is still a problem for many regions around the world, and identifying whether or not the vaccine course is necessary after a bite means that thousands are yet susceptible to contracting rabies. Once symptoms appear, the disease progresses rapidly, and in clinical settings has a listed fatality rate of 100 percent, making rabies the single most fatal infectious disease in the world (Jackson et al., 2003; Willoughby et al., 2005; Susilawathi et al., 2012; Tarantola, 2017).

If, at this time, you are wondering why a disease with a 100 percent fatality rate is being featured in a book focused on survival and recovery from neurotrauma, then here is where the twenty-first century steps in. In 2004, a 15-year-old girl was bitten on the hand by a bat that she had attempted to rescue after it struck a window inside of her neighborhood church. The bite did not seem serious, so her parents cleaned the cut with peroxide and thought nothing more of it until she began to show signs of illness (Willoughby et al., 2005; Lite, 2008). In the absence of the post-exposure vaccination, the rabies virus can lie dormant for weeks, occasionally for as long as two years, depending on how distant from the brain the offending bite takes place (Susilawathi et al., 2012). In Jeanna Giese's case, where the bite was sustained on the hand, the delay lasted nearly a month. Common symptoms of early clinical rabies are rather nondescript, including fatigue, nausea and vomiting, numbness or weakness of limbs, and headache, any one of which can be misinterpreted as other diagnoses (Willoughby et al., 2005; CDC, 2009; Susilawathi et al., 2012). After developing fatigue and tingling in the left hand, double vision appeared, closely followed by nausea, loss of motor control, and rapid progression of central nervous system symptoms. In addition to Giese's symptoms of ataxia (loss of movement coordination), tremors, and speech disruptions, many others identified as having clinical rabies also experience confusion, excitability, and hypersalivation (Susilawathi et al., 2012). If agitation symptoms are prevalent, it is characterized as furious rabies; if paralysis and weakness is more prevalent, as in Giese, then paralytic rabies is diagnosed. For her, this was five days into symptom development, far too late to administer the post-exposure vaccine course, and well into the average five to seven-day timepoint at which most victims' stories end (Willoughby et al., 2005). The next day, the CDC confirmed the presence of rabies-specific antibodies in cerebrospinal fluid and blood serum. Her parents were told to expect the worst, but gave permission to attempt a yet unvalidated course of treatment involving induction of a therapeutic coma and intensive care.

Under careful monitoring of all body systems, sedatives such as ketamine were administered to induce a therapeutic coma under the hopes that removing the strain of maintaining her failing body would allow her immune system time to kick into high gear and speed up the production of antibodies to fight off the infection (Willoughby et al., 2005). Amantadine, a compound known to reduce excitotoxicity or overactivity of neural systems, was added in to support the immune system's fight against the virus. Miraculously, despite the constant need of life-support systems and intensive care, signs of recovery began to appear about a week after the induction of the coma. Hypersalivation, the origin of the 'foaming at the mouth' associated with rabies, decreased as viral antibodies continued to increase in the bloodstream. A medication-resistant fever spiked, but responded to a change in whole room temperature. Finally, the sedatives were tapered off, and she slowly and gradually regained consciousness responding to tests and manipulations. By the time her breathing tube was removed, nearly a month after admission to the hospital, she could understand what was going on around her and express genuine and appropriate emotions. Physical therapy rehabilitation helped her get back on her feet, speech therapy guided her restored communication, and within five months, she was going back to school. She had officially become the first documented person in the world to have survived clinical rabies without a single administration of the post-exposure vaccine.

While out of the woods at last, Giese's recovery was far from complete. She worked hard with regular physical therapy and speech therapy, and was left with some partial paralysis on the left side, but made an amazing recovery (Lite, 2008; Razner, 2019). Ever grateful to have survived the ordeal, she is dedicated to spreading awareness of the disease and encouraging the use of the 100 percent effective preventative vaccines. But as to exactly *why* she survived, the outcome is not so optimistic, but rather enigmatic. The intensive course of treatment she received was dubbed the Milwaukee Protocol, and while only experimental, her success gave it credence and it would be further attempted in other cases of rabies considered to be beyond the 'point of no return'.

The Milwaukee Protocol

Since its introduction in 2005, the protocol that saved the life of the first rabies survivor has received a fair amount of criticism, but is far from being abandoned. Instead, it is being refined. Like any other medical innovation, bugs need to be worked out, treatments included need to be adjusted or swapped out, and individual needs need to be taken into consideration. Critics cite its first survivor as the only one, though the protocol's lead contributor, Dr. Willoughby, estimates the survival rate as high as 20 percent,[2] and Giese herself has encouraged further refinement and continued research into the technique.

One of the major goals of the Milwaukee Protocol is to control the dangerous levels of autonomic dysfunction in clinical rabies, though some critics argue that not all cases have such extreme levels of disruption (Aramburo et al., 2011; Zeiler & Jackson, 2016). Support for this argument appears in the form of rabies survivors who have not required intensive care, though the often-cited Texas case in 2009 included administration of a single dose of the vaccine, the possibility of an alternate form of *Lyssavirus* as opposed to true rabies, and an undetermined final outcome of the patient (CDC, 2009). Another case from 1970 investigates a small child that received a bite from a rabid bat, but did not himself show positive anti-rabies antibodies until *after* receiving a two week course of the vaccine almost immediately after being bitten (Hattwick et al., 1972). Authors of the report from this case acknowledged that it is possible the boy was experiencing an extremely rare form of post-vaccination encephalitis, and though they attest that rabies contraction was far more likely, it remains unclear whether or not it was a true case of clinical rabies.

Mechanistically, the Milwaukee Protocol approaches excitotoxicity, or cell death due to overactivity, with amantadine, an antagonist of NMDA, the main receptor type for the neurotransmitter glutamate (Willoughby et al., 2005). Complete blockade of the receptor, however, may actually interfere with the immune system and its ability to clear bacterial infections, and its impact on viral infections is yet unknown (Zeiler & Jackson, 2016). Its use should therefore include an exercise of caution, as should the use of sedatives for initiating the therapeutic coma. Willoughby and colleagues certainly acknowledge that their existing protocol is far from perfected, that it may only even be an option for as little as 10 percent of affected patients, and that fatality rates are still too high (Lite, 2008; Aramburo et al., 2011). Yet in the absence of an alternative protocol, and by integrating new and ongoing research findings, it is as of now the best option available to those who present signs of clinical rabies without access to the vaccines. It further experienced another success with adaptations in 2011 when a child in California showed symptoms as long as four to nine weeks after being scratched by feral cats near her school (Carollo, 2011; CDC, 2012). Experiencing paralytic symptoms like the case in Wisconsin, no vaccine was administered, but sedatives and autonomic support guided the young patient through gradual recovery with minimal long-lasting effects, and cementing her place as the third documented case of surviving clinical rabies without any vaccine administration.

Future Research

While the case presented here and its successive survivors are especially exciting and encouraging after millennia of death and doom, rabies remains a terrifying problem to much of the world.

Many areas have limited, if any, access to the preventative or post-exposure prophylactic vaccines, and even in advanced nations, the cost of the course can be extreme (as much as ten times the cost as in developing nations) (Lite, 2008). The Milwaukee Protocol and other adaptations will therefore remain necessary, and their refinement is certainly needed. In light of arguments against the protocol, examinations of the exact actions of the rabies virus in the brain still need to be performed, and the exact role of glutamate and NMDA receptors narrowed down. At this time, it appears that the goal of maintaining the brain's existing health through therapeutic sedation and intense supportive care warrants more exploration. We can therefore hope and strive to see a day within our current lifetimes where rabies encephalitis is removed from the top of the world's 'most fatal' list of infectious neurotoxic diseases.

Notes

1   It is uncertain if this attempt to weaponize Rabies was successful or not.
2   While this number may seem quite low compared to other procedures, it is important to note that this is compared to the 0 percent survival rate in untreated rabies.

Chapter 14

'Down like a Ton of Bricks'

Iron Mike Webster and Chronic Traumatic Encephalopathy

No Helmet Thick Enough

Mike Webster broke a lot of records during his relatively short life. Escaping poverty from rural Wisconsin, Webster won accolades in bowling as well as being a prolific American football player, earning four Super Bowl rings, the love of the entire city of Pittsburg, and numerous other athletic records. He is said to have played in more pro football games than any other player for his National Football League (NFL) team, the Steelers: 220 games, not including games played with other teams or on school teams (Laskas, 2015). He died at 50 years old of an apparent heart attack. But it is the list of odd behaviors he displayed prior to his death that led one stubborn neuropathologist to ask questions and uncover an entire undiscussed category of brain degeneration: chronic traumatic encephalopathy (CTE).

Webster retired from football at the age of 38 and spent more time with his loving family, his wife, Pam, and four children. The family bought a new house and was happy for a time. Gradually, though, Webster changed. He became easily angered and could not control his temper. His memory was full of gaps that grew larger and larger. He was tired a lot, and lost money but could not remember how it had been lost. One day, he peed in the oven.[1] He was in constant pain, was losing his teeth (but would attempt to super-glue them back into place), and began wandering aimlessly while muttering and even waving firearms around. He lived in his car or in hotels, and would taser himself into unconsciousness to get some sleep. People generally assumed that he had gone insane. At times of clarity, he knew that something had gone deeply wrong with him, but he had no way of knowing what it was. He sought the help of a lawyer to get the NFL, as his former employers, to help pay for his disability and health care, but was turned down several times. And so it was that he was found dead, estranged from his family and in dire need of help that he would never receive. And he was far from the only person suffering so.

Doctor Bennet Omalu, a determined immigrant from Nigeria with numerous advanced degrees, was studying under famed pathologist Cyril Wecht in Pittsburg when Mike Webster's body came into his morgue for a routine autopsy. Not being into many sports (other than European football/soccer), he had no idea who the man was, other than that he had been in the news and everyone around him was shocked to hear of his death. But he knew about the game he played, and could plainly see how badly beaten up and scarred the man's body was. He was certain that if the game could do such dramatic damage to Webster's body, his brain must also have been a complete wreckage. However, upon removing the brain and examining it, Omalu found no obvious signs of damage, not even the contusions that are commonly present after sustaining a concussion. Stunned, he ordered his technician to preserve the brain so he could dive deeper into the details.

While the gross appearance of Webster's brain appeared normal, the micropathology, or microscopic signs of damage, showed otherwise. Before his death, Webster's behaviors showed signs of mood disorders, cognitive dysfunction, and Parkinsonism. Microscopically, Omalu found amyloid plaques and tau protein tangles, both typically associated with Alzheimer's disease, pallor or loss of cells in the substantia nigra, a trademark of Parkinson's disease, and thinning of cells throughout the brain (Omalu et al., 2005). Both Alzheimer's and Parkinson's are degenerative conditions that do not commonly appear until an individual is in their 60s or older, yet Webster was only in his 40s when he began to show symptoms. He had no family history of either disease to explain early onset of dementia, so the only reasonable explanation at this point had to be repetitive damage due to his career as an athlete in high-impact sports. As the first clearly identifiable case, Omalu named it CTE: Chronic to represent its consistent impact on daily life, Traumatic to emphasize the role of concussions and brain damage, and Encephalopathy to highlight the pathology within the brain. To make things worse, all other players in the NFL were likely also at risk of developing CTE as Webster did, so more research into it was absolutely necessary.

When Omalu opened up Webster's brain, he also opened a massive can of worms, stirring up the ire of the NFL, who insisted repeatedly that the game was not causing brain damage. They brought up their own panel of 'experts', none of whom were neuropathologists, and all of whom were paid by the league and possessed conflicts of interest (Laskas, 2015). A public battle would ensue, eerily reminiscent of the tobacco industry when they had denied the link between smoking and cancer. Football was causing early-onset dementia, and the NFL was not taking responsibility for it, or even warning their players of the risks, revoking their ability to make informed decisions about their own long-term welfare.

Almost as soon as the controversy around Omalu's publications began, more cases of former football players dying young with dementia symptoms began to appear. Terry Long, a colleague of Webster's, killed himself at age 45 after three previous failed attempts at suicide and over 13 years of struggling with depression and other symptoms. Andre Waters from the Philadelphia Eagles put a gun in his mouth at age 44 after years of pain and had even had a seizure on the field while playing. Justin Strzelczyk, also from the Steelers, had severe memory and mood disturbances as well as depression and paranoia, vanishing for days to weeks at a time, and eventually killing himself at age 36 by driving head-on into a truck filled with corrosive acid. Tom McHale of the Tampa Bay Buccaneers overdosed on oxycodone and cocaine at 45. Owen Thomas played with the University of Pennsylvania after playing school and extramural football since age 9, hanging himself in his apartment at the age of 21 despite not having been officially diagnosed with concussions during his time as a player. Fred McNiell of the Minnesota Vikings survived thoughts of suicide, but just barely, being placed in an in-patient facility for such severe memory disruptions that he could not remember a phone call from his wife five minutes earlier; he was 55 when institutionalized, and passed away in 2015 at the age of 63, after which an autopsy confirmed that he had been the first living diagnosis of CTE on record. Dave Duerson from the Chicago Bears shot himself in the chest at age 50, leaving a note specifically stating that his brain was to be donated to the study of CTE; nobody had known how much he had struggled before then. Finally, Junior Seau of the San Diego Chargers, beloved by fans not only of football but also of his TV show and other ventures, shot himself in the chest at age 43 in the same way as Duerson had. And these are just the cases contained in Omalu's story, *Concussion* (Laskas, 2015). The rate of suicide alone should have been enough to raise suspicions and initiate investigations into mental illness in athletes.

Despite the NFL's resistance to the idea, more and more research teams began exploring CTE after Omalu's identification of the disorder. Former players have expressed that had they known about the risk of neurological disorder, they would not have played, and they certainly would not allow their kids to play. Enrollment in peewee football for young kids dropped dramatically. Out of a single study including 111 brains donated by former NFL players, 110 of those were confirmed as showing pathology consistent with CTE (Ward et al., 2017). Signs of CTE have been identified in high school football players and boxing as well (McCrory et al., 2007; Reinberg, 2019). Various sub-types of CTE have been categorized, and diagnostic criteria refined (Montenigro et al., 2014). Forced to acknowledge the issue, the NFL agreed to make changes to standard procedures, such as education and sideline management of concussive symptoms (NFL, 2019). College and high school teams enacted guidelines for when to allow players to re-enter the game after sustaining a blow to the head, though regulations for this are loose and allow for manipulation.[2]

While padding and helmets are designed specifically to protect players and prevent excess injuries, they are not yet effective at preventing the development of CTE. Smaller sub-concussive hits such as those sustained by linemen may not lead to identifiable concussions, but may build up to create subtler, widespread damage, much like a transient ischemic attack compared to a larger stroke. Omalu had once suggested that the helmets themselves may even be serving as a sort of weapon, allowing harder hits and more intracranial shifting of the brain (Laskas, 2015). This suggestion was further supported when a player in 2019 used an opponent's helmet as a literal weapon, smashing the helmet over his head during a dispute (Garcia & Mather, 2019). Therefore, as we make changes and develop new technology, it is essential to continue exploring the finer details of CTE, learning to delineate it from other disorders and identify the offending events that contribute to it.

Parallels to and Risks of Other Diseases

At its first identification, CTE showed immediate parallels to other neurological conditions. Omalu and a colleague both agreed that Webster's brain pathology looked like a case of advanced Alzheimer's disease (Omalu et al., 2005; Laskas, 2015). They further connected it to an older, but likely identical, disorder that was well-known to fans and athletes in boxing: dementia pugilistica. Also known as 'punch drunk syndrome', dementia pugilistica was named after boxers (pugilists), its most common victims, as it was suspected that being punched in the head repeatedly was not good for your brain. Who knew? Common effects of dementia pugilistica were memory loss, cognitive disruptions, and hearing issues, potentially even hallucinations. It was such a well-known effect that it was even a comedy bit in Red Skelton's act as the classic character, Cauliflower McPugg,[3] a punch-drunk boxer with slurred speech who frequently heard birds and bells. As late as 2007, a confirmed case of dementia pugilistica was shown to overlap significantly with other forms of neurological degeneration such as Alzheimer's and Parkinson's disease (Areza-Fegyveres et al., 2007). The parallels between compound concussive damage and other forms of degeneration are too strong to ignore, emphasizing a need to differentiate between CTE and other disease states (McKee et al., 2013).

Alzheimer's Disease. From the onset of its exploration, Omalu noted similarities between Webster's sample and typical Alzheimer's cases. While not a perfect fit, the tau protein pathology that is highly correlated to Alzheimer's symptoms was dense and widespread in Webster's brain. Typically a functionally helpful compound, in disease states, the tau protein becomes hyperphosphorylated and collects into tangle-like structures that interfere with brain function and contribute to cell death (McKee et al., 2013). Omalu had previously examined a 44-year-old woman's brain who had died after being beaten into a coma by an abusive spouse, and found it to be filled with the same tau pathology (Laskas, 2015). Like with Alzheimer's, pathology tends to be particularly dense in the hippocampus, the main memory center of the brain, connected areas like the entorhinal cortex, and includes whole brain atrophy (Areza-Fegyveres et al., 2007; Stern et al., 2011; McKee et al., 2013).

CTE differs from Alzheimer's though in many ways, including the lack of beta-amyloid plaques, one of the trademark pathologies of Alzheimer's disease, and often a diagnostic requirement (Stern et al., 2011; McKee et al., 2013). The age of onset for each is significantly different, with typical sporadic Alzheimer's beginning as young as the early 60s and later, and CTE affecting age ranges from the 20s to the 80s. Former boxers have been recorded as having increased risk of Alzheimer's disease or similar dementias, though recent links to the Apolipoprotein E (APOE) gene may better explain the predisposition to neurological complications and prolonged recovery from trauma (Stern et al., 2011). Further, only a small portion of boxers who developed degenerative symptoms matched criteria for Alzheimer's diagnoses, showing more connections to motor deficits such as those seen in Parkinson's disease (McCrory et al., 2007).

Parkinsonism and Lewy Body Disease. Outside of neurological circles, the line between Parkinson's disease and Parkinsonism gets blurred. Within medical and scientific fields, however, they are considered to be completely different conditions. Parkinson's disease is a unique degenerative disorder characterized by rigidity (bradykinesia) and tremors, dopamine cell loss in the substantia nigra, and many other troubling symptoms (Langston & Palfreman, 1995). Parkinsonism, on the other hand, describes a collection of motor symptoms in absence of true Parkinson's disease, including the rigidity and tremors, dyskinesias (uncontrolled movements), trouble starting and stopping voluntary movements, and episodes of freezing. In cases of CTE, Parkinsonism appears both physically and pathologically. The substantia nigra, the dopamine-rich area deep within the midbrain that is damaged in Parkinson's disease, shows pallor or loss of color in CTE, as does the locus coeruleus, a brainstem area associated with stress responses (McCrory et al., 2007; Stern et al., 2011). The presence of Lewy bodies, clumps of alpha-synuclein expressing proteins, in these brainstem areas are further indicative of disease states, and may contribute to cell death in the dopamine system (Beyer et al., 2009). In a comprehensive study comparing CTE to other disease states, over a third of patients examined had a comorbid diagnosis, 16 percent of whom were also consistent with Lewy body disease (McKee et al., 2013). Of other motor-system diseases, such as amyotrophic lateral sclerosis (ALS), another 12 percent fit the diagnostic criteria. Yet the connections between repetitive head trauma and motor symptoms are less surprising to those familiar with CTE's ancestor, dementia pugilistica, which begs the question of who else should be added to the list of at-risk populations for developing these degenerative disease states.

At-Risk Individuals

While recent studies have focused primarily on high-impact sports like boxing and American football as contributors to CTE, they are certainly not the only relevant risk factors. The details of an individual's time in the game may also be relevant to their risks and rates of progress. For instance, boxers traditionally would participate in frequent bouts with no protective headgear, and were seen to have a higher risk of dementia if they had sustained blows that knocked them unconscious or produced post-concussive symptoms (McCrory et al., 2007). People have often joked that only the boxers who were bad at the game developed dementia, so it was met with some reluctance to admit that when beloved pugilist Mohamed Ali developed pronounced Parkinson's disease, it may have, in fact, been due to his long and successful career (Park, 2016).

Connections between a person's type of athletics and their CTE sub-types may be further illustrated with a look at different types of brain trauma. As with Ali, many boxers went on to develop motor symptoms, potentially connected to rotational forces, as a blow to the head causes it to rotate, sheering axons in critical regions responsible for voluntary movement, and even the deep brainstem areas associated with Parkinsonism (Stern et al., 2011; McKee et al., 2013; Montenigro et al., 2014). In contrast, American football players tend to take more head-on blows to the front of the head, which is reflected in a higher rate of Alzheimer's-like symptoms. Within the sport as well is a difference between linemen and quarterbacks, as one position features the bashing of tackles and the other more frequent sub-concussive hits. These sub-concussive hits, which produce micro-traumas with no immediately recognizable symptoms, often go unnoticed until the damage is too far gone to reverse, and suggest that there are entire other populations affected by CTE that we have not identified yet. Other groups studied for the effects of repeated head injuries have included hockey and rugby players, military veterans, and autistic and self-harming individuals, the latter of which illustrate the importance of studying frequent sub-concussive hits.[4] These varieties have led to suggestions for standardized diagnostic criteria and sub-types of CTE such as mood variants and cognitive variants

(Montenigro et al., 2014). Military service members, too, are subject to sub-concussive hits, not as often from direct contact comparatively, but from blast waves. Those with multiple tours of duty are at higher risk of developing symptoms. A new model of traumatic injury, the fluid percussion model, seeks to replicate these blast injuries by transmitting a shock wave through a fluid-filled cylinder and into the head of experimental subjects. Though still being optimized as of 2020, the model shows great promise as a way of testing repetitive head trauma and its effects on cognitive and motor symptoms.

Future Directions

More changes are critically needed to protect American football players from brain damage, though fans of the game insist that it will not be the same without tackles and linemen. Yet the rules have changed before, such as when legendary sportsman Teddy Roosevelt urged changes such as the legalization of the forward pass and breakup of mass formations, changes that reduced the number of fatalities per year to 11 between 1906 and 1907 (Klein, 2012). Just as we are developing better armor for the men and women who serve in our militaries, it would be wise to develop better prevention methods for contact sports. As much as Americans love the game of football, it isn't necessarily worth the damage it does to the players and their lives.

Still ongoing, increasing numbers of scientists are exploring new fields of Sports Medicine and Exercise Science, not only geared towards orthopedics and bodily injuries incurred by athletics, but now also encompassing head impacts and the identification of small-scale concussions that can often be missed. Others still are refining helmets and instituting consequences when a player fouls against another. Surely, as we develop greater understanding for CTE and other delayed trauma-related illnesses, we shall also continue to develop better ways to protect our athletes, soldiers, and children from such fates.

Notes

1 Unlike Phineas Gage's reportedly peeing on a house plant at a dinner party, Webster's urination story was verified, and began to scare and worry his children.

2 While teaching a university class, a student once came to me and explained how their coach taught them to play dumb during their pre-season cognitive assessments so that they would not be removed from the game after being impaired by a blow to the head. If they looked stupid before, then being rendered dumb by a concussion would not appear on a test ... I was appalled, and of course reported it to a supervisor, only to hear nothing back as follow-up.

3 The character name of Cauliflower McPugg is also a clever pun: Cauliflower to represent 'cauliflower ears', a visible sign of cartilage damage when opponents strike or pull on the ears; and McPugg as a shortened adaptation of the term pugilist.

4 There has also been a recorded case of a circus performer who served as a human cannonball so many times that he, too, developed CTE (reported in Stern et al., 2011).

Chapter 15

'Misery Loves Company'

Similarities among Highly Variable TBIs/SCIs

Comorbidity

There is a common idiom that states that bad things tend to happen in sets of threes. While the actual rate of misfortune may vary based on interpretation, there also is no denying that bad things seldom occur alone. In science and medicine, the occurrence of more than one disease state at the same time is known as comorbidity. Many forms of mental and neurological illnesses are comorbid with one another, such as Huntington's disease and emotional dysfunction, strokes and aphasias, and depression and basically any other disease state. Neurotrauma is no exception to the rule, and often results in overlaps between individual cases. As such, various cases of traumatic brain and spinal cord injuries may be both vastly different and reasonably similar at the same time. Understanding these similarities may improve predictability, allowing us to better communicate what the victims of neurotrauma may be at an increased risk for during the course of their recoveries. Therefore, let us praise that which connects us yet again, and discuss how we can use these common threads to help one another.

Seizures

As you may have already noticed, seizures and epilepsy have been a repetitive subject throughout the presented cases of head injuries. Post-traumatic seizures were reported by cultures practicing trephination,[1] were responsible for the untimely death of Phineas Gage, affected Louis Leborgne long before his fateful stroke, were a likely factor in the epilepsy that led to Henry Molaison's memorable operation, occurred throughout James

Brady's recovery, and were even recorded in NFL players with potential CTE. Incidence rates have an extremely wide range, estimated as occurring in as low as 2.6 percent or as high as 53 percent of TBI victims, with higher estimates ascribed to injured war veterans (Frey, 2003; Szaflarski et al., 2014; Ding et al., 2016). One potential explanation for the increased incidence of post-traumatic seizures in soldiers is the type of injury sustained. A rodent model of TBI known as fluid percussion, which mimics the blast injuries of modern warfare, is found to be sufficient to produce seizures after only a single impact (D'Ambrosio et al., 2004). Exploration into whether or not the meninges are damaged during human injuries found increased rates of seizure activity when the dura was penetrated, further connecting epidemiology to the severity of the injury. Translated into plain English, it seems that the more severe and penetrating a TBI, the higher the risk for developing post-traumatic epilepsy.

Pain

It may seem like a no-brainer that getting bashed in the head can lead to headaches, yet the details of pain after neurotrauma spread wider than expected. Aside from the expected acute pain immediately after being injured, post-traumatic pain can occur long after the insult, reappear again at later times, and may be constant or chronic, as in Roald Dahl's severe and career-changing headaches. Headache alone may happen in as much as 95 percent of those who sustain a TBI, even one as mild as a concussion, and will evolve into a full-blown migraine in two-thirds of those cases (Hoffman et al., 2011; AMF, 2018). Like with seizures, veterans are at an increased risk of post-traumatic headaches, potentially compounded due to the stress of military service. Connections have been found between post-traumatic headaches and brain areas affected, as well as with inflammation, which may further relate to other forms of post-traumatic pain (Mayer et al., 2013; Schwedt et al., 2017).

Neuropathy as a whole refers to a disorder due to nerve damage, and most often is used to refer to pain and numbness in the hands and feet. Yet neuropathy is strikingly common post-injury in those with brain and spinal cord injuries. Post-traumatic pain has been linked to inflammation, errant signaling in damaged or disconnected nerve cells, and even particular cell and receptor sub-types (Yawn et al., 2009; Ji et al., 2013; Smith, 2014; Matyas et al., 2017a). In some cases, damage to one region of the CNS may lead to neuropathy in distant areas far from the focal point of the damage, including the hands and feet, or the cranial nerves. This type of pain typically does not respond well to traditional pain management, but has shown some promise when treated with tricyclic antidepressants and anticonvulsant medications. Experimental treatments for neuropathy attempt to identify more effective therapies by targeting specific factors, such as inhibition of NOX2, an enzyme involved in the inflammatory and anti-inflammatory processes of microglia (Sabirzhanov et al., 2019). Because neuropathy may begin as tingling sensations and progress to sharp pain, or may even remain as tingling or numbness, it is important to discuss any altered sensations with caregivers and medical professionals as symptoms appear.

Memory Loss

Memory is incredibly fragile even in healthy, uninjured individuals. It can even be manipulated intentionally, as shown by the groundbreaking work of Dr. Elizabeth Loftus. After a head injury, memory becomes even more fragile.[2] To some degree, post-traumatic amnesia extending after and shortly before an injury may be a normal, protective effect so the person does not remember a time period of pain and discomfort. The length and extent of amnesia can even be used as a diagnostic factor, since it directly relates to the severity of damage (Kolb & Wishaw, 2009; Pinel & Barnes, 2018). Memory loss that extends beyond the acute post-traumatic period is often less severe than the complete absence of memory, but is nonetheless frustrating to those forced to deal with it on a daily basis. In a healthy hippocampus, long-term potentiation (LTP) has been strongly linked to the formation of new memories, and may be compromised after an injury, leading to difficulties in memory consolidation. Depending on the severity of the problem, a person may get along fine by using additional sticky notes around the house, or may have so much difficulty that they require assistance with complex tasks. Proper identification of post-traumatic memory disturbances must take place under the supervision of a trained professional, who can then also arrange a proper treatment plan appropriate to the individual's needs.

A Case to Tie Them All Together – Mike from Michigan

In 1990, a truck driver and business owner was hauling lumber in central Michigan, and while tying down his load, the gravity cock broke, sending the tie-down bar soaring upwards through his head. Until this moment, Mike's memory is very clear, but at the moment of the impact, everything had to be filled in by others who were present at the scene (Krakker, 2019). In a story reminiscent of Phineas Gage, the metal bar punctured his face at the upper lip, continuing through his skull and out the other end, missing the brain by just a hair's breadth. He was thrown an estimated 15 feet into the air, landing hard with a blow to the back of his head, and woke up propped against a post with his leather gloves pressed against his bleeding face. While the bar itself did not actually puncture the brain, the shock of the blow coupled with falling onto the back of his head had a clear and permanent effect on Mike's life. Almost immediately after having emergency surgery (his left maxillary sinus is now completely gone, and a sliver of bone still remains inside of the brain case), Mike began having seizures almost daily while asleep.

Though only a few of his seizures were categorized as grand mal, each one ended with an intense post-ictal headache, which he described as feeling 'like an all-night drunk' episode. Medications keep the seizures under control, but they are not a perfect solution, and the occasional sudden-onset seizure can occur with little to no warning. Fortunately, Mike has access to a magnificent warning system that alerts him to when he needs to take emergency medication to prevent these sudden seizures: his therapy dog, Gizmo. Professionally trained in Lansing, Gizmo is able to detect subtle changes that act as warning signs for an oncoming seizure, and when he detects them, he will whine and demand attention from Mike 15 minutes before the seizure would begin. When there is no imminent threat, Gizmo happily stays seated on his own box accepting pats and words of admiration.[3] Between Gizmo's warnings and management with medications, Mike's seizures are almost completely controlled. Yet there are other factors that prohibit him from returning to work as he would like.

Aside from seizures, Mike also experiences a few very common effects from his injury: lateral neuropathy, memory loss, and vertigo. The neuropathy he describes is less of a pain sensation than a pins-and-needles type of tingling, which affects his entire right side at all times; the side opposite his original injury. He has no loss of sensation or mobility on that side, though, and has also had two vertebrae partially removed to relieve symptoms of degenerating discs, much like in the case of Roald Dahl. More troublesome though is the impact of his injuries on his memory. Describing his pre-injury memory as photographic, Mike used to be able to draw out blueprints from memory alone. Compared to that, his memory is now essentially gone. Physical therapy required him to relearn walking, writing, and other basic tasks, but the loss of his strong memory distress him more. Finally, Mike lives with an effect not extensively discussed in the present text but nonetheless equally as common as his other maladies: vertigo.

For many people who have not experienced recurrent vertigo, the name evokes a classic Hitchcock movie of the same title starring Jimmy Stewart, who plays a man with a severe fear of heights. Far from being directly related to the phobia, however, vertigo is shown in the spinning sensation experienced during the man's phobic episodes, and more accurately describes a sense of dizziness, imbalance, and instability. Fear and anxiety may trigger a bout of vertigo, but so too can regular stress, drugs and alcohol, fatigue, dehydration, caffeine consumption, improper blood flow, rapid changes in body position, and a myriad of other benign stimuli. Those living with chronic conditions like Meniere's disease and benign paroxysmal positional vertigo (BPPV) will also trigger an episode seemingly randomly by doing such daring things as looking up or turning their head too fast or too far to one side. Types of vertigo are often identified based on their triggers as well as basic characteristics of the episode, such as the presence of nystagmus, or involuntary eye movements. In Mike's case, his symptoms match other types of positional vertigo, in that he is unable to tilt his head up or turn too quickly without setting off an attack, and must use a cane to help maintain his balance. Over a level surface, the cane may not be necessary, yet the moment one's plane of existence must shift, as in bending over to pick up an item off the floor, all sense of balance flies out the window. This makes returning to work problematic, and further throws off the sense of depth perception, which was already compromised for Mike.

Throughout the decades that Mike has lived with his post-injury self, he remains upbeat and positive. His personality is still his own, and he maintains a number of hobbies and has healthy relationships with others. Far from considering himself a victim, Mike is a person with a fascinating story to tell. Sharing his story with others and spotting the similarities he shares with other cases acts as a sort of morbid group therapy, providing social support and encouragement to others who experience TBIs of their own. Telling your own story may be difficult at first; there is no denying that you have been through something traumatic. But once you are ready to share it, there will be others there to listen and to share their own stories in return, and through our shared misery, we will be better able to help and support one another, and come up with new solutions to the problems that plague survivors of neurotrauma.

Closing Remarks and Thanks

Of the thousands of horrible things that can happen to a person, nothing gets quite the same gasp as the announcement of a brain injury or a broken neck. The terms themselves carry grim prognoses, and very often can prove fatal. However, amongst the thorns lie a rose, and amid the tragedies of neurotrauma lie new bits of knowledge and learning. Without such cases as those discussed here, we would know little to nothing about the human brain, nor how to help people when something goes wrong with it. It is therefore appropriate now to show the deepest gratitude to those who were willing to share their stories with us so that we may learn from them. Thanks to these people, we have learned so much about how the brain operates in regard to personality, emotions, speech, memory, movement, sensation, and many other subjects.

If you or somebody you know has sustained damage to the brain or spinal cord, know that there is *always* a chance for recovery. Nobody can read your future and tell you whether or not you can regain what you've lost. Your case is not outlined by textbooks, but is unique to you. There may be patterns that arise between your case and others, yet there will also be differences that change the way you approach your recovery. Decades ago, we believed the idea Cajal put forth stating that the brain and spinal cord do not regenerate after damage; we now know that was not true. The limitations we had then are no longer as difficult to overcome. Similarly, the limitations that we have today may someday no longer be a problem. The things we feel constrained by now we may someday see are wrong. Therefore, look forward, and keep moving toward the future. The research will be right there alongside you.

Notes

1 Cultural trephination practices are thought to have been traditionally done in attempts to alleviate seizures, including both spontaneous seizures in children and post-traumatic seizures in adults, suggesting a potential bidirectional relationship between brain damage and the occurrence of seizures.
2 Memory becomes more fragile after injury with the exception of acquired synesthesia, in which memory tends to become stronger and more precise.
3 Gizmo gets a lot of admiration as well, because he is a very good boy. He stays seated on his box until told to get down, and gets noticeably upset if Mike leaves the room without him.

References

Aaron, B. & Rockoff, D. 1994. The attempted assassination of President Reagan: medical implications and historical perspective. *JAMA*, 272. 1689–1693.

ABC News. 2012. Face-eating cannibal attack may be latest in string of 'bath salts' incidents. *In:* ABC News (ed.). [Online]. abcnews.go.com.

Ahmed, A. & Simmons, Z. 2013. Pseudobulbar affect: prevalence and management. *Ther Clin Risk Manag, 9*, 483–489.

Akiyama, T., Mccoy, B., Go, C. Y., Ochi, A., Elliott, I. M., Akiyama, M., Donner, E. J., Weiss, S. K., Snead, O. C., 3RD, Rutka, J. T., Drake, J. M. & Otsubo, H. 2011. Focal resection of fast ripples on extraoperative intracranial EEG improves seizure outcome in pediatric epilepsy. *Epilepsia, 52*, 1802–1811.

American Migraine Foundation. 2018. Concussion, migraine & post-traumatic headache. Accessed through on August 18, 2019 www.ameri canmigrainefoundation.org.

Annese, J., Schenker-Ahmed, N. M., Bartsch, H., Maechler, P., Sheh, C., Thomas, N., Kayano, J., Ghatan, A., Bresler, N., Frosch, M. P., Klaming, R. & Corkin, S. 2014. Postmortem examination of patient H. M.'s brain based on histological sectioning and digital 3D reconstruction. *Nat Commun, 5*, 3122.

Anonymous. 2017. *RE: Personal Communication.* Type to Matyas, J.

Anonymous. 2019. *RE: Personal Communication.* Type to Matyas, J.

APA. 2013. *Diagnostic and Statistical Manual of Mental Disorders*, Washington, D.C., USA: American Psychiatric Association (APA).

Aramburo, A., Willoughby, R. E., Bollen, A. W., Glaser, C. A., Hsieh, C. J., Davis, S. L., Martin, K. W. & Roy-Burman, A. 2011. Failure of the Milwaukee protocol in a child with rabies. *Clin Infect Dis, 53*, 572–574.

Areza-Fegyveres, R., Rosemberg, S., Castro, R., Porto, C., Bahia, V., Caramelli, P. & Nitrini, R. 2007. Dementia pugilistica with clinical features of Alzheimer's disease. *Arq Neuropsiquiatr, 65*, 830–833.

Asadi-Pooya, A. A., Sharan, A., Nei, M. & Sperling, M. R. 2008. Corpus callosotomy. *Epilepsy Behav*, 13, 271–278.

Aschner, M. & Aschner, J. L. 1990. Mercury neurotoxicity: mechanisms of blood-brain barrier transport. *Neurosci Biobehav Rev*, 14, 169–176.

ASHA. 2020. *American Speech-Language-Hearing Association* [Online]. www.asha.org. [Accessed 2020].

Bakheit, A., Shaw, S., Carrington, S. & Griffiths, S. 2007. The rate and extent of improvement with therapy from the different types of aphasia in the first year after stroke. *Clin Rehabil*, 27, 941–949.

Balcells, M. 2014. The history of leucotomy. *Neurosciences and History*, 3, 130–135.

Bandelier, A. F. 1904. Aboriginal trephining in Bolivia. *Am Anthropol*, 6, 440–446.

Benabid, A., Chabardes, S., Mitrofanis, J. & Pollak, P. 2009. Deep brain stimulation of the subthalamic nucleus for the treatment of Parkinson's disease. *Lancet Neurol*, 8, 67–81.

Benevento, B. T. & Sipski, M. L. 2002. Neurogenic bladder, neurogenic bowel, and sexual dysfunction in people with spinal cord injury. *Phys Ther*, 82, 601–612.

Bey, T. & Patel, A. 2007. Phencyclidine intoxication and adverse effects: a clinical and pharmacological review of an illicit drug. *The California Journal of Emergency Medicine*, 8, 9–14.

Beyer, K., Domingo-Sabat, M. & Ariza, A. 2009. Molecular pathology of Lewy body diseases. *Int J Mol Sci*, 10, 724–745.

Bigelow, H. 1850. Case of injury of head. *Am J Med Sci*, 39, 2–22.

Bons, D., Van Den Broek, E., Scheepers, F., Herpers, P., Rommelse, N. & Buitelaar, J. K. 2013. Motor, emotional, and cognitive empathy in children and adolescents with autism spectrum disorder and conduct disorder. *J Abnorm Child Psychol*, 41, 425–443.

Borders, C., Hsu, F., Sweidan, A. J., Matei, E. S. & Bota, R. G. 2018. Deep brain stimulation for obsessive compulsive disorder: a review of results by anatomical target. Ment Illn, 10, 1–13.

Brady, J. S. 2011. Jim Brady, 30 years later. *In:* Simon, S. (ed.). (national public radio).

Brainobservatory, T. 2018. *Patient H M* [Online]. www.thebrainobserva tory.org/project-hm. [Accessed] January 2020.

British Medical Journal. 2000. Doctors warn of the dangers of trepanning. *British Medical Journal*, 320, 602.

Broca, P. 1861. Remarks on the seat of the faculty of articulated language, following an observation of aphemia (loss of speech) – translated from French to English by C.D. Green (2000). *Bulletin de la societe anatomique*, 6, 330–357.

Broca, P. 2011. On the site of the faculty of articulated speech (1865). *Neuropsychol Rev*, 21, 230–235.

Carey, B. 2008. H.M., an unforgettable amnesiac, dies at 82. *The New York Times*.

Carollo, K. 2011. California girl only third in us to survive rabies without vaccine. *Abc News Medical Unit*.

Caruso, J. P. & Sheehan, J. P. 2017. Psychosurgery, ethics, and media: a history of Walter Freeman and the lobotomy. *Neurosurg Focus*, 43, E6.

Carvalho, C. M., Chew, E. H., Hashemy, S. I., Lu, J. & Holmgren, A. 2008. Inhibition of the human thioredoxin system. A molecular mechanism of mercury toxicity. *J Biol Chem*, 283, 11913–11923.

CDC. 2009. Presumptive abortive human rabies – Texas, 2009. *Morb Mortal Wkly Rep*, 59, 1–6.

CDC. 2012. Recovery of a patient from clinical rabies – California, 2011. *Morb Mortal Wkly Rep*, 61.

CDRF. 2019. *Actor, Director, and Activist* [Online]. www.christopher reeve.org. [Accessed] January 2020.

Cenci, M. A. & Lundblad, M. 2005. Utility of 6-Hydroxydopamine lesioned rats in the preclinical screening of novel treatments for Parkinson disease. *In:* Mark LeDoux (ed.).*Animal Models of Movement Disorders*, Elsevier. 193–208.

Check Hayden, E. 2011. Anatomy of a brain injury. *Nature*. 1–3.

Cho, N., Squair, J. W., Bloch, J. & Courtine, G. 2019. Neurorestorative interventions involving bioelectronic implants after spinal cord injury. *Bioelectron Med*, 5, 1–19.

Cimons, M. 1995. Reeve injury called among worst possible. *LA Times*.

Clower, W. T. & Finger, S. 2001. Discovering trepanation: the contribution of Paul Broca. *Neurosurgery*, 49, 1417–1425.

Collado-Vázquez, S. & Carrillo, J. M. 2014. Cranial trepanation in The Egyptian. *Neurología (English Edition)*, 29, 433–440.

Colton, M. 1998. You need it like … a hole in the head? If you're looking for enlightenment, here's the drill. *The Washington Post*.

Corkin, S. 2013. *Permanent Present Tense*, New York, NY, Basic Books.

Corrosion Doctors. 2019. *Mad as a Hatter* [Online]. corrosion-doctors.org. [Accessed] November 2019.

Cytowic, R. 1981. The long ordeal of James Brady. *The New York Times Magazine*.

D'Ambrosio, R., Fairbanks, J. P., Fender, J. S., Born, D. E., Doyle, D. L. & Miller, J. W. 2004. Post-traumatic epilepsy following fluid percussion injury in the rat. *Brain*, 127, 304–314.

Dahl, R. 1986. Measles: a dangerous illness. *Roald Dahl Fans: Essays and Articles* [Online].

Damasio, H., Grabowski, T., Frank, R., Galaburda, A. & Damasio, A. 1994. The return of Phineas Gage: clues about the brain from the skull of a famous patient. *Science*, 264: 5162, 1102–1105.

Dargelos. 1888. *Process of Preparing Animal-hairs for Felting*. France patent application.

Dashti, S. R., Baharvahdat, H., Spetzler, R. F., Sauvageau, E., Chang, S. W., Stiefel, M. F., Park, M. S. & Bambakidis, N. C. 2008. Operative intracranial infection following craniotomy. *Neurosurg Focus*, 24, E10.

Dateline. 2019. *Hinckley: Diary of a Dangerous Mind*.

Dauer, W. & Przedborski, S. 2003. Parkinson's disease: mechanisms and models. *Neuron*, 39, 889–909.

Ding, K., Gupta, P. & Diaz-Arrastia, R. 2016. Epilepsy after traumatic brain injury. *In:* Laskowitz, D. & Grant, G. (eds.). *Translational Research in Traumatic Brain Injury*, Boca Raton, FL, CRC Press.

Dolan, R. J. 2007. Keynote address: revaluing the orbital prefrontal cortex. *Ann N Y Acad Sci*, 1121, 1–9.

Donovan, D., Moquin, R. & Ecklund, J. 2006. Cranial burr holes and emergency craniotomy: review of indications and technique. *Mil Med*, 171, 12–19.

Doran, J. 2016. I drilled a hole in the skull to stay high forever. *Vice*.

Dronkers, N. F., Plaisant, O., Iba-Zizen, M. T. & Cabanis, E. A. 2007. Paul Broca's historic cases: high resolution MR imaging of the brains of Leborgne and Lelong. *Brain*, 130, 1432–1441.

Dully, H. & Fleming, C. 2007. *My Lobotomy*, New York, NY, Crown Publishing Group.

El-Hai, J. 2005. *The Lobotomist*, Hoboken, NJ, John Wiley & Sons, Inc.

Faleiro, R. M., Faleiro, L. C. M., Caetano, E., Gomide, I., Pita, C., Coelho, G., Bras, E., Carvalho, B. & Gusmao, S. N. S. 2008. Decompressive craniotomy. *Arq Neuropsiquiatr*, 66, 369–373.

Faria, M. A., Jr. 2013. Violence, mental illness, and the brain – a brief history of psychosurgery: part 1 – from trephination to lobotomy. *Surg Neurol Int*, 4, 49.

Faria, M. A. 2015. Neolithic trepanation decoded – a unifying hypothesis: has the mystery as to why primitive surgeons performed cranial surgery been solved? *Surg Neurol Int*, 6, 72.

Ferrier, D. 1878a. Goulstonian lectures on the localisation of cerebral disease – Lecture 1 (concluded). *BMJ*. 443–447.

Ferrier, D. 1878b. Goulstonian lectures on the localisation of cerebral disease – Lecture 2. *BMJ*. 471–476.

Follett, K. A., Weaver, F. M., Stern, M., Hur, K., Harris, C. L., Luo, P., Marks, W. J., Rothlind, J., Sagher, O., Moy, C., Pahwa, R., Burchiel, K., Hogarth, P., Lai, E. C., Duda, J. E., Holloway, K., Samii, A., Horn, S., Bronstein, J. M., Stoner, G., Starr, P. A., Simpson, R., Baltuch, G., De

Salles, A., Huang, G. D. & Reda, D. J. 2010. Pallidal versus subthalamic deep-brain stimulation for Parkinson's disease. *New England Journal of Medicine*, 362, 2077–2091.

Frey, L. 2003. Epidemiology of posttraumatic epilepsy: a critical review. *Epilepsia*, 44, 11–17.

Friberg, L. 1991. Environmental health criteria 118: inorganic mercury. World Health Organization.

Friedman, J. H. & Fernandez, H. H. 2005. Drug-induced movement disorders. *In: Animal Models of Movement Disorders*, London UK: Elsevier Academic Press. 713–724.

Ganey, T. M., Hutton, W. C., Moseley, T., Hedrick, M. & Meisel, H. J. 2009. Intervertebral disc repair using adipose tissue-derived stem and regenerative cells. *Spine*, 34, 2297–2304.

Ganey, T. M. & Meisel, H. J. 2002. A potential role for cell-based thereapeutics in the treatment of intervertebral disc herniation. *Eur Spine Journal*, 11, S206–S214.

Garcia, O. & Mather, V. 2019. Browns' Myles Garrett suspended indefinitely for hitting Mason Rudolph with Helmet. *The New York Times*.

Getz, M. J. 2009. The ice pick of oblivion: Moniz, Freeman and the development of psychosurgery. *Trames J Humanit Soc Sci*, 13, 129–152.

Gilbert, A. 2018. The relationship between pesticides and Parkinson's. Accessed November 2019 American Parkinson Disease Association, adpaparkinson.org.

Gislason, T. B., Sjogren, M., Larsson, L. & Skoog, I. 2003. The prevalence of frontal variant frontotemporal dementia and the frontal lobe syndrome in a population based sample of 85 year olds. *J Neurol Neurosurg Psychiatry*, 74, 867–871.

Gnanalingham, K., Lafuente, J., Thompson, D., Harkness, W. & Hayward, R. 2002. Surgical procedures for posterior fossa tumors in children: does craniotomy lead to fewer complications than craniectomy? *J Neurosurg*, 97, 821–826.

Gorgey, A. S. 2018. Robotic exoskeletons: the current pros and cons. *World J Orthop*, 9, 112–119.

Gross, C. 2009. *A Hole in the Head*, Cambridge, MA, The MIT Press.

Guanziroli, E., Cazzaniga, M., Colombo, L., Basilico, S., Legnani, G. & Molteni, F. 2019. Assistive powered exoskeleton for complete spinal cord injury: correlations between walking ability and exoskeleton control. *Eur J Phys Rehabil Med*, 55, 209–216.

Hader, W. J., Tellez-Zenteno, J., Metcalfe, A., Hernandez-Ronquillo, L., Wiebe, S., Kwon, C. S. & Jette, N. 2013. Complications of epilepsy surgery: a systematic review of focal surgical resections and invasive EEG monitoring. *Epilepsia*, 54, 840–847.

Hans, V. & Slater, D. 1983. John Hinckley, Jr. and the insanity defense: the public's verdict. *Cornell Law Faculty Publications*.

Harkema, S., Gerasimenko, Y., Hodes, J., Burdick, J., Angeli, C., Chen, Y., Ferreira, C., Willhite, A., Rejc, E., Grossman, R. G. & Edgerton, V. R. 2011. Effect of epidural stimulation of the lumbosacral spinal cord on voluntary movement, standing, and assisted stepping after motor complete paraplegia: a case study. *The Lancet*, 377, 1938–1947.

Harlow, John M. 1868. Recovery after severe injury to the head. *Massachusetts Medical Society*.

Haskin, A., Kim, N. & Aguh, C. 2016. A new drug with a nasty bite: a case of krokodil-induced skin necrosis in an intravenous drug user. *JAAD Case Rep*, 2, 174–176.

Hattwick, M., Weis, T., Stechschulte, J., Baer, G. & Gregg, M. 1972. Recovery from rabies: a case report. *Ann Intern Med*, 76, 931–942.

Henderson, G. L. 1988. Designer drugs: past history and future prospects. *J Forensic Sci*, 33, 569–575.

Hermann, P. & Ruane, M. 2014. Medical examiner rules James Brady's death a homicide. *The Washington Post*.

Hoffman, J. M., Lucas, S., Dikmen, S., Braden, C. A., Brown, A. W., Brunner, R., Diaz-Arrastia, R., Walker, W. C., Watanabe, T. K. & Bell, K. R. 2011. Natural history of headache after traumatic brain injury. *J Neurotrauma*, 28, 1719–1725.

Horsley, V. 1888. Trephining in the neolithic period. *The Journal of the Anthropological Institute of Great Britain and Ireland*, 17, 100–106.

Houle, J. D. & Cote, M. P. 2013. Axon regeneration and exercise-dependent plasticity after spinal cord injury. *Ann N Y Acad Sci*, 1279, 154–163.

Howard, K. 2016. Question: did Dahl ever speak publicly or write about his brain injury? *Roald Dahl Fans: General Dahl News* [Online].

Hubbard, E. M. & Ramachandran, V. S. 2005. Neurocognitive mechanisms of synesthesia. *Neuron*, 48, 509–520.

Jackson, A., Warrell, M., Rupprecht, C., Ertl, H., Dietzschold, B., O'reilly, M., Leach, R., Fu, Z., Wunner, W., Bleck, T. & Wilde, H. 2003. Management of rabies in humans. *Clin Infect Dis*, 36, 60–63.

Jackson-Lewis, V. & Smeyne, R. J. 2005. From man to mouse: the MPTP model of Parkinson disease. *In: Animal Models of Movement Disorders*, London UK: Elsevier Academic Press. 149–160.

Jacobs, J. & Potter, K. 1995. Keeping guns out of the wrong hands: the Brady law and the limits of regulation. *J Crim Law Criminol*, 86, 93–120.

Ji, R. R., Berta, T. & Nedergaard, M. 2013. Glia and pain: is chronic pain a gliopathy? *Pain*, 154, Suppl 1, S10–28.

Johnson, G. S. 2016. Roald Dahl's brain damage may have contributed to his work. *Brain Injury* [Online].

Kalat, J. 2013. *Biological Psychology*, Belmont, CA, Wadsworth.

Kalat, J. 2019. *Biological Psychology*, Boston, MA, Cengage.

Kjellberg, R. & Prieto, A. 1971. Bifrontal decompressive craniotomy for massive cerebral edema. *J Neurosurg*, 34, 488–493.

Klein, C. 2012. How Teddy Roosevelt saved football. *History Stories*. The History Channel.

Kolb, B. & Wishaw, I. Q. 2009. *Fundamentals of Human Neuropsychology*, New York, NY, Worth Publishers.

Krakker, F. M. 2019. Interview with the author. *In:* Matyas, J. (ed.).

Krassioukov, A., Warburton, D. E., Teasell, R. & Eng, J. J. & Spinal Cord Injury Rehabilitation Evidence Research Team. 2009. A systematic review of the management of autonomic dysreflexia after spinal cord injury. *Arch Phys Med Rehabil*, 90, 682–695.

Lanczik, M. & Keil, G. 1991. Carl Wernicke's localization theory and its significance for the development of scientific psychiatry. *Hist Psychiatry*, 2, 171–180.

Langston, J. W. & Palfreman, J. 1995. *The Case of the Frozen Addicts*, New York, NY, Random House, Inc.

Laskas, J. M. 2015. *Concussion*, New York, NY, Random House.

Lee, W. R. 1968. The history of the statutory control of mercury poisoning in Great Britain. *Brit J Industrial Med*, 25, 52–62.

Lite, J. 2008. Medical mystery: only one person has survived Rabies without vaccine – but how? *Scientific American*.

Lorch, M. 2011. Re-examining Paul Broca's initial presentation of M. Leborgne: understanding the impetus for brain and language research. *Cortex*, 47, 1228–1235.

Mallin, R. & Rathbun, T. 1976. A Trephined Skull from Iran. *Bull NY Acad Med*, 52, 782–787.

Mathews, M. S., Linskey, M. E. & Binder, D. K. 2008. William P. van Wagenen and the first corpus callosotomies for epilepsy. *J Neurosurg*, 108, 608–613.

Matyas, J. 2012. *The Effects of Mesenchymal Stem Cells on Disc Structure in a Rat Caudal Model of Intervertebral Disc Degeneration*. Master of Sciences, Central Michigan University.

Matyas, J. J., O'Driscoll, C. M., Yu, L., Coll-Miro, M., Daugherty, S., Renn, C. L., Faden, A. I., Dorsey, S. G. & Wu, J. 2017a. Truncated TrkB.T1-mediated astrocyte dysfunction contributes to impaired motor function and neuropathic pain after spinal cord injury. *J Neurosci*, 37, 3956–3971.

Matyas, J. J., Stewart, A. N., Goldsmith, A., Nan, Z., Skeel, R. L., Rossignol, J. & Dunbar, G. L. 2017b. Effects of bone-marrow-derived MSC transplantation on functional recovery in a rat model of spinal cord injury: comparisons of transplant locations and cell concentrations. *Cell Transplant*, 26, 1472–1482.

Mautes, A., Weinzierl, M., Donovan, F. & Noble, L. 2000. Vascular events after sci: contribution to secondary pathogenesis. *Phys Ther*, 80, 17.

Mayer, C. L., Huber, B. R. & Peskind, E. 2013. Traumatic brain injury, neuroinflammation, and post-traumatic headaches. *Headache*, 53, 1523–1530.

McCrory, P., Zazryn, T. & Cameron, P. 2007. The evidence for chronic traumatic encephalopathy in boxing. *Sports Med*, 37, 467–476.

McKee, A. C., Stern, R. A., Nowinski, C. J., Stein, T. D., Alvarez, V. E., Daneshvar, D. H., Lee, H. S., Wojtowicz, S. M., Hall, G., Baugh, C. M., Riley, D. O., Kubilus, C. A., Cormier, K. A., Jacobs, M. A., Martin, B. R., Abraham, C. R., Ikezu, T., Reichard, R. R., Wolozin, B. L., Budson, A. E., Goldstein, L. E., Kowall, N. W. & Cantu, R. C. 2013. The spectrum of disease in chronic traumatic encephalopathy. *Brain*, 136, 43–64.

Meisel, C., Schwab, J. M., Prass, K., Meisel, A. & Dirnagl, U. 2005. Central nervous system injury-induced immune deficiency syndrome. *Nat Rev Neurosci*, 6, 775–786.

Miller, A., Pratt, H. & Schiffer, R. B. 2011. Pseudobulbar affect: the spectrum of clinical presentations, etiologies and treatments. *Expert Rev Neurother*, 11, 1077–1088.

Mohammed, N., Narayan, V., Patra, D. P. & Nanda, A. 2018. Louis Victor Leborgne ("Tan"). *World Neurosurg*, 114, 121–125.

Montenigro, P., Baugh, C. M., Daneshvar, D. H., Mez, J., Budson, A. E., Au, R., Katz, D. I., Cantu, R. C. & Stern, R. A. 2014. Clinical subtypes of chronic traumatic encephalopathy: literature review and proposed research diagnostic criteria for traumatic encephalopathy syndrome. *Alzheimer's Res Ther*, 6, 1–17.

NAA. 2020. *Aphasia Definitions* [Online]. www.aphasia.org/aphasia-def initions. [Accessed 2020].

Neufeld, J., Roy, M., Zapf, A., Sinke, C., Emrich, H. M., Prox-Vagedes, V., Dillo, W. & Zedler, M. 2013. Is synesthesia more common in patients with Asperger syndrome? *Front Hum Neurosci*, 7, 847.

Neylan, T. C. 1999. Frontal Lobe function: Mr. Phineas Gage's famous injury. *J Neuropsychiatry Cln Neuroscience*, 11, 280–283.

NFL. 2019. *Football Operations* [Online]. operations.nfl.com. [Accessed] February 2020.

Nishimura, Y., Iwai, T., Kobayashi, N., Tsuji, F., Toyama, O. & Nakamura, M. 2013. Time-dependent changes in the microenvironment of injured spinal cord affects the therapeutic potential of neural stem cell transplantation for spinal cord injury. *Mol Brain*, 6, 1–15.

Nix, E. 2018. Where did the phrase "mad as a hatter" come from? *In:* Channel, T. H. (ed.). *History Stories.* New York, NY, USA. Accessed online June 15, 2019.

Norenberg, M., Smith, J. & Marcillo, A. 2004. The pathology of human spinal cord injury: defining the problems. *J Neurotrauma*, 21, 429–440.

Ojemann, G., Ojemann, J., Lettich, E. & Berger, M. 1989. Cortical language localization in left, dominant hemisphere. An electrical stimulation mapping investigation in 117 patients. *J Neurosurg*, 71, 316–326.

Ojo, O. A., Poluyi, E. O., Owolabi, B. S., Kanu, O. O. & Popoola, M. O. 2017. Surgical decompression for traumatic spinal cord injury in a tertiary center. *Niger J Clin Pract*, 20, 1455–1460.

Omalu, B. I., Dekosky, S. T., Minster, R. L., Kamboh, M. I., Hamilton, R. L. & Wecht, C. H. 2005. Chronic traumatic encephalopathy in a National Football League player. *Neurosurgery*, 57, 128–134, discussion 128-34.

OSHA. 1970. Occupational safety and health standards: occupational health and environmental control. *Hazard Communication Standard (USA).* Public Law 91-596, enacted December 29, 1970, amended through January 1, 2004. Washington D.C., USA.

Padgett, J. 2016 Presidential lecture. National Neurotrauma Society Lexington, KY.

Padgett, J. & Seaberg, M. 2014. *Struck by Genius: How a Brain Injury Made Me a Mathematical Marvel*, New York, NY, Houghton Mifflin Harcourt Publishing Company.

Park, A. 2016. The complicated link between Muhammad Ali's death and boxing. *Time Health.*

Pedersen, P. M., Vinter, K. & Olsen, T. S. 2004. Aphasia after stroke: type, severity and prognosis. The Copenhagen aphasia study. *Cerebrovasc Dis*, 17, 35–43.

Perlmutter, J. & Tabbal, S. 2005. MPTP-induced nigrostriatal injury in nonhuman primates. *In: Animal Models of Movement Disorders*, London UK: Elsevier Academic Press. 139–148.

Pfeiffer, R. F. 2005. The phenotypic spectrum of Parkinson disease. *In: Animal Models of Movement Disorders*, London UK: Elsevier Academic Press. 127–137.

Pinel, J. P. & Barnes, S. J. 2018. *Biopsychology*, Hoboken, NJ, Pearson.

Ramachandran, V. S. & Hubbard, E. M. 2003. The phenomenology of synaesthesia. *J Conscious Stud*, 10, 49–57.

Ratiu, P., Talos, I. F., Haker, S., Lieberman, D. & Everett, P. 2004. The tale of Phineas Gage, digitally remastered. *J Neurotrauma*, 21, 637–643.

Razner, S. 2019. 15 years after she survived rabies, Jeanna Giese seeks to save others from it. *FDL Reporter.*

Reagan, R. 1991. Why I'm for the Brady Bill. *The New York Times.*

Reinberg, S. 2019. Brain condition CTE found in HS football players. *Health Day* [Online].

Rosenzweig, D. H., Carelli, E., Steffen, T., Jarzem, P. & Haglund, L. 2015. 3D-Printed ABS and PLA scaffolds for cartilage and nucleus pulposus tissue regeneration. *Int J Mol Sci*, 16, 15118–15135.

Rosenzweig, E. S. & McDonald, J. W. 2004. Rodent models for treatment of spinal cord injury: research trends and progress toward useful repair. *Curr Opin Neurol*, 17, 121–131.

Sabirzhanov, B., Li, Y., Coll-Miro, M., Matyas, J. J., He, J., Kumar, A., Ward, N., Yu, J., Faden, A. I. & Wu, J. 2019. Inhibition of NOX2 signaling limits pain-related behavior and improves motor function in male mice after spinal cord injury: participation of IL-10/miR-155 pathways. *Brain Behav Immun*, 80, 73–87.

Sahjpaul, R. 2000. Awake craniotomy: controversies, indications and techniques in the surgical treatment of temporal lobe epilepsy. *Can J Neurol Sci*, 27, 55–63.

Schiffer, R. & Pope, L. 2005. Review of pseudobulbar affect including a novel and potential therapy. *J Neuropsychiatry Cln Neuroscience*, 17, 447–454.

Schwedt, T. J., Chong, C. D., Peplinski, J., Ross, K. & Berisha, V. 2017. Persistent post-traumatic headache vs. migraine: an MRI study demonstrating differences in brain structure. *J Headache Pain*, 18, 87.

Scoville, W. B. & Milner, B. 1957. Loss of recent memory after bilateral hippocampal lesions. *J Neurol Neurosurg Psychiat*, 20, 11–21.

Selnes, O. A. & Hillis, A. 2000. Patient tan revisited: a case of atypical global aphasia? *J Hist Neurosci*, 9, 233–237.

Sibai, B. M. 1990. Magnesium sulfate is the ideal anticonvulsant inpreeclampsia-eclampsia. *Am J Obstet Gynecol*, 162, 1141–1145.

Simpson, D. 2005. Phrenology and the neurosciences: contributions of F. J. Gall and J. G. Spurzheim. *ANZ J Surg*, 75, 475–482.

Smith, B. 2014. *What Is Neuropathic Pain* [Online]. International Association for the Study of Pain. [Accessed December 2019].

Solomon, T. 2016. How family tragedy turned Roald Dahl into a medical pioneer. *The Guardian* [Online].

Stehr-Green, P., Tull, P., Stellfeld, M., Mortenson, P.-B. & Simpson, D. 2003. Autism and thimerosal-containing vaccines. *Am J Prev Med*, 25, 101–106.

Stern, R. A., Riley, D. O., Daneshvar, D. H., Nowinski, C. J., Cantu, R. C. & Mckee, A. C. 2011. Long-term consequences of repetitive brain trauma: chronic traumatic encephalopathy. *PM R*, 3, S460–467.

Stewart, A. N., Matyas, J. J., Welchko, R. M., Goldsmith, A. D., Zeiler, S. E., Hochgeschwender, U., Lu, M., Nan, Z., Rossignol, J. & Dunbar, G. L. 2017. SDF-1 overexpression by mesenchymal stem cells enhances GAP-43-positive axonal growth following spinal cord injury. *Restor Neurol Neurosci*, 35, 395–411.

Sturrock, D. 2010. *Storyteller, the Authorized Biography of Roald Dahl*, New York, NY, Simon & Schuster Paperbacks.

Susilawathi, N. M., Darwinata, A. E., Dwija, I. B., Budayanti, N. S., Wirasandhi, G. A., Subrata, K., Susilarini, N. K., Sudewi, R. A., Wignall, F. S. & Mahardika, G. N. 2012. Epidemiological and clinical features of human rabies cases in Bali 2008–2010. *BMC Infect Dis*, 12, 1–8.

Szaflarski, J. P., Nazzal, Y. & Dreer, L. E. 2014. Post-traumatic epilepsy: current and emerging treatment options. *Neuropsychiatr Dis Treat*, 10, 1469–1477.

Tanriverdi, T., Olivier, A., Poulin, N., Andermann, F. & Dubeau, F. 2009. Long-term seizure outcome after corpus callosotomy: a retrospective analysis of 95 patients. *J Neurosurg*, 110, 332–342.

Tarantola, A. 2017. Four thousand years of concepts relating to rabies in animals and humans, its prevention and its cure. *Trop Med Infect Dis*, 2, 1–21.

Taubman, P. 1981. Investigators think Hinckley Stalked Carter. *The New York Times*.

Teive, H., Munhoz, R. & Caramelli, P. 2011. Historical aphasia cases. *Arq Neuropsiquiatr*, 69, 555–558.

Tello Velasquez, J., Ekberg, J. A. K. & St John, J. A. 2015. Transplantation of olfactory ensheathing cells in spinal cord injury. *In:* Zhao L.R., Zhang J. (eds.) *Cellular Therapy for Stroke and CNS Injuries*. Springer Series in Translational Stroke Research. Springer, Cham. Springer, Cham.

Torregrossa, M., Quinn, J. & Taylor, J. 2008. Impulsivity, compulsivity, and habit: the role of the orbitofrontal cortex revisited. *Biol Psychiatry*, 63, 253–255.

Treffert, D. A. 1999. The savant syndrome and autistic disorder. *CNS Spectr*, 4, 57–60.

Treffert, D. A. 2009. The savant syndrome: an extraordinary condition. A synopsis: past, present, future. *Philos Trans R Soc Lond B Biol Sci*, 364, 1351–1357.

Van den Broeck, K. 2018. What did hat makers (hatters) use mercury for?.

Van Horn, J. D., Irimia, A., Torgerson, C. M., Chambers, M. C., Kikinis, R. & Toga, A. W. 2012. Mapping connectivity damage in the case of Phineas Gage. *PLoS One*, 7, e37454.

van Wagenen, W. P. & Herren, R. Y. 1940. Surgical division of commissural pathways in the corpus callosum: relation to spread of an epileptic attack. *Arch Neurol Psychiatry*, 44, 740–759.

Von Delpech, H. 1874. A method of preparing the fur of rabbits and hares for the manufacture of felt without the use of mercury. *Technical Chemistry*, 27, 99.

Ward, J., Schnakenberg, P. & Banissy, M. J. 2018. The relationship between mirror-touch synaesthesia and empathy: new evidence and a new screening tool. *Cogn Neuropsychol*, 35, 314–332.

Ward, J., Williams, J. & Manchester, S. 2017. 110 NFL brains. *The New York Times*.

Watters, D. 2007. Skull trepanation in the Bismarck Archipelago. *PNG Med J*, 50, 20–24.

WHL. 2019. Rosemary Kennedy *Project Gutenberg* [Online].

Williams, S. S. 2016. The terrorist inside my husband's brain. *Neurology*, 87, 1308–1311.

Willoughby, R., Tieves, K., Hoffman, G., Ghanayem, N., Amlie-Lefond, C., Schwabe, M., Chusid, M. & Rupprecht, C. 2005. Survival after treatment of rabies with induction of coma. *New England Journal of Medicine*, 352, 2508–2514.

Yawn, B. P., Wollan, P. C., Weingarten, T. N., Watson, J. C., Hooten, W. M. & Melton, L. J., 3RD. 2009. The prevalence of neuropathic pain: clinical evaluation compared with screening tools in a community population. *Pain Med*, 10, 586–593.

Zabramski, J., Kiris, T., Sankhla, S., Cabiol, J. & Spetzler, R. 1998. Orbitozygomatic craniotomy. *J Neurosurg*, 89, 336–341.

Zeiler, F. A. & Jackson, A. C. 2016. Critical appraisal of the Milwaukee protocol for rabies: this failed approach should be abandoned. *Can J Neurol Sci*, 43, 44–51.

Zilles, K. & Amunts, K. 2010. Centenary of Brodmann's map–conception and fate. *Nat Rev Neurosci*, 11, 139–145.

Index